Tropospheric Politics

The History of the Amendments to the Constitution: A Political Etiology

Darryl Murphy

The Author of Three Blind Mice

ISBN: 1514898152
ISBN 13: 9781514898154
Library of Congress Control Number: 2015913696
CreateSpace Independent Publishing Platform
North Charleston, South Carolina

Table of Contents

Chapter 1

❧

Introduction

Tropospheric Politics is a follow up to my first book **Three Blind Mice** which tells the story of the three Presidents before Lincoln and the decade of the 1850s. I think it's important to continue the discussion of people and decisions that helped to shape the United States of America the world knows in the Twenty-First Century. What is Tropospheric Politics? Simply put, it's the politics we live and conduct on the ground. The layer of Earth's atmosphere where all seven billion human beings live, except for the occasional crazy fucking astronaut. Earth's atmosphere has five layers to it. Those layers are the troposphere, the stratosphere, the mesosphere, the thermosphere, and the exosphere. Aerologists define the troposphere as existing from sea level to seven miles into the atmosphere. The stratosphere exists from seven to thirty one miles up. The mesosphere goes from thirty one to fifty miles. The thermosphere, from fifty miles to four hundred forty miles and the exosphere anything greater than four hundred forty miles. Different things happen at different "spheres." For instance, commercial aircraft typically fly within the troposphere or about thirty five thousand feet. The much discussed ozone layer sits within the stratosphere. The International Space Station orbits Earth within the thermosphere or about two hundred and fifty miles up. So "Tropospheric Politics" is where we practice politics, by definition.

When the Constitution of the United States was written the framers knew that no one could live by just those words and only those words in perpetuity. Thusly, they allowed for a little wiggle room for changing times. That wiggle room shows itself in the form of the Amendments to the United States Constitution.

Today, if you asked the average person who is even remotely interested in the subject, they would tell you there are twenty seven amendments to the United States Constitution. However, there are actually thirty three amendments of which twenty seven have been ratified by the requisite number of states. How an amendment comes to be is unique in itself. When it comes to how laws are originated, debated, passed and enacted in the United States its process is the only one that doesn't require the signature of the President of the United States.

It's unique; because the process of an amendment becoming a law, in effect, makes the states a defacto "fourth" branch of government. Because of this one could say that the four branches of government are the Executive, Legislative, Judicial and the individual States as a collective body. Although rarely discussed, this is the purity of the phrase in the Declaration of Independence "of the people, for the people, by the people."

The Founding Fathers were smart enough to set up a two way process to amend anything they may have left out in the day-to-day lives of the way every American legally lived. An amendment can start in either the United States House of Representatives or the United States Senate.

Once passed by both houses of the United States Congress with a two thirds majority it is sent for ratification by the individual states. For an amendment to become law it requires three-fourths of the states to comply. Today that is thirty eight of the fifty states. On the other hand, the process can start from the state level as well. In this case, if only two-thirds of the states agree on a piece of legislation, they can force a constitutional convention to be held for the United States Congress to consider an amendment. Although, this has never occurred, if it did it would be taken very seriously in Washington, D.C. The first thing a Congressman or Congresswoman uses to defend their position is "my constituents feel this way." So, they would be hard pressed to ignore a direct appeal from the collective voice of the states themselves. That is, if they wanted to be re-elected. There has been plenty written about the United States Constitution and the amendments to the document and some of that will be re-hashed here. What will also be discussed are the effects of the amendments on the history of the United States of America.

Throughout the book I will examine the origins of the amendments, the players behind each and give examples, both good and bad on how they affect the lives of all Americans.

Chapter 2

✒

Article Five of the United States Constitution

Article Five of the United States Constitution is the vehicle that allowed for slack to be taken in on the oversized pants that is the United States Constitution. It says either the United States Congress or the individual states themselves can draw language on an amendment. Article Five allowed the Founding Fathers an "out," plain and simple.

Chapter 3

❦

The Six that Didn't Make The Cut

O f the thirty three amendments to the United States Constitution
six of them never became law. Four are still pending and two died
(as a result of sunset language), never to raise their heads again.

The six were as follows; The Congressional Apportionment
Amendment, Titles of Nobility Amendment, Corwin Amendment,
Child Labor Amendment, Equal Rights Amendment and the District of
Columbia Voting Rights Amendment. The four are still pending (offi-
cially), the two latter failed.

The Congressional Apportionment Amendment was all about how
many individuals from each state should represent the "people" in
Washington, D.C. In this case they First United States Congress settled
on one representative for every fifty thousand people. Based on current
population numbers, if this amendment would have passed today there
would be around six thousand members in the United States House of
Representatives. If you think shit doesn't get done now just imagine

that scenario. The idea of the amendment was to have some kind of minimum representation for the common people and, at the same time limit the size of electoral districts. The Congressional Apportionment Amendment is also called Article the First, because, it was literally the first amendment passed and sent to the states for ratification. Even before what became the Bill of Rights. So the Bill of Rights was supposed to be a twelve amendment compilation. The state legislatures decided to discard the first two and keep the other ten. Ironically, the other amendment that didn't pass, Article the Second, eventually became the Twenty-Seventh Amendment to the United States Constitution some two hundred years later. But we'll get to that. Because there is no deadline for state ratification, the Congressional Apportionment Amendment is still pending and could still be enacted if passed by the requisite number of current states in the Union (today, thirty eight of the fifty states).

Only eleven state legislatures have ratified the amendment. These are the states of New Jersey, Maryland, North Carolina, South Carolina, New Hampshire, New York, Connecticut, Rhode Island, Vermont and the Commonwealths of Pennsylvania, Kentucky and Virginia. The next amendment, not to be ratified by the minimum number of states legislatures (but still pending) is the Titles of Nobility Amendment or TONA. This amendment would have stripped United States citizenship from anyone accepting a title of nobility from a foreign country. Its purpose was to keep states from offering titles of nobility to its citizens. It was proposed in 1810 by United States Senator Philip Reed of Maryland during a session of the Eleventh United States Congress. Philip Reed served as a Captain in the American Revolutionary War. Reed was not a man to be fucked with. He served in the battles of Stony Point and Camden.

Hard on deserters he even cut a soldier's head off and had it displayed so others would get the point.

After the American Revolutionary War he served in the Maryland House of Delegates and was also sheriff of Kent County, Maryland. He also served as a Lieutenant Colonel of the Maryland Militia during the War of 1812. He also served as Vice President of the Maryland Society of the Cincinnati. The Society of the Cincinnati is a hereditary lineage organization, established for officers who served in the Continental Army and Navy during the American Revolutionary War. So it's ironic that Senator Reed would propose a bill with exclusionary language. However, part of his motivation was the actions of one of his own constituents. The marriage of Baltimore resident Elizabeth "Betsy" Patterson to Jerome Bonaparte caused quite a stir on both sides of the Atlantic Ocean. Betsy took to calling herself, and others referred to her, as the "Duchess of Baltimore." Jerome Bonaparte was the younger brother of Napoleon Bonaparte. Jerome met Betsy when he visited the United States. Funny thing about all of this is big bro Napoleon didn't think much of the marriage. He set out to sabotage that shit from the giddy up.

He ordered his brother back to France and tried to have the marriage annulled. Napoleon even denied Betsy entry into continental Europe. She would eventually end up in London where she would give birth to a son also named Jerome Napoleon Bonaparte. His birth and this "title" bullshit would be another reason Senator Reed would bring the Titles of Nobility Amendment to the floor of the United States Senate for consideration. Nobody could figure out what the fuck to call this kid. He was born in England to an American mother and his father, who was Napoleon's brother! Napoleon would eventually get his way with his brother, as Betsy would return to Baltimore, Maryland and Jerome would become a bigamist and royal at the same time when he married Catharina of Wurttemberg while still married to Betsy (although they would ultimately divorce). States legislatures that voted for ratification were Maryland, Ohio, Delaware, New Jersey, Vermont, Tennessee, North Carolina, Georgia, New Hampshire and the Commonwealth legislatures of Pennsylvania, Kentucky and Massachusetts. The State legislatures of New York, Connecticut and Rhode Island would reject the amendment.

One could speculate that the patriotic nature of this amendment would have definitely passed had, it not been for the outbreak of the War of 1812. The lead up to the war and the subsequent hostilities quickly change political priorities in Washington, D.C. This would be the country's first attempt at passing a Thirteenth Amendment to the United States Constitution. When we talk about war and national law the Corwin Amendment was a direct attempt to avoid war. Plainly the Corwin Amendment was Washington, D.C.'s way of saying to the South, "if you don't secede we won't fuck with you guys over the slavery issue and we'll put it in writing." The actual text reads; No amendment shall be made to the Constitution which will authorize or give to Congress the power to abolish or interfere, within any State, with the domestic institutions thereof, including that of persons held to labor or service by the laws of said State. Imagine if this amendment had actually been ratified by the required number of states. This one amendment would have changed the course of American history, and I am not sure for the better.

Between his election in 1860 and taking office in March, 1861 Abraham Lincoln made several attempts to avert war through compromise and after South Carolina's secession, diplomacy. The Corwin Amendment, like the Crittenden Compromise was an effort too little, too late for many in the South. As well as just being fed up with the North, many Southerners just wanted to fight for fighting sake. The greed of Southern plantation owners was just the deadly sin that fucked them up the ass and at the same time the best thing to happen to Black people in America. If the Corwin Amendment had become the Thirteenth Amendment to the United States Constitution, several events don't happen. Timeline is important for this discussion. Before the Corwin Amendment there was the Crittenden Compromise. Introduced by then Commonwealth of Kentucky Senator John J. Crittenden on December 18, 1860, it was a "package" of legislative proposals designed to pacify the South and a serious attempt to avoid fighting. Remember, sitting President James Buchanan is a lame duck President and Abraham Lincoln, as President-Elect doesn't take office until March, 1861. Also, only two days later the State of South Carolina would officially secede from the Union on December 20, 1861.

Mix in the political combustion that is Washington, D.C., political divisions were deep and hardcore. As a result, the United States Congress wasn't just split between the United States House of Representatives and the United States Senate. It wasn't just split between Republicans and Democrats either. It was now split between pro-slavery and abolitionists, secessionists and Union preservationists and North and South. Introducing the Crittenden Compromise and the Corwin Amendment was like the guy who buys his wife a vacuum cleaner for her Valentine's Day gift. He thinks he's being creative and thoughtful but he didn't know he only added accelerate to that fire. On top of all of this was the lingering effect of the real first battle of the Civil War fought on May 22, 1856. A battle won by the South and rather decisively. The setting of the battle was the United States Senate chamber at the United States Capitol. The belligerents were United States Congressman Preston Brooks of South Carolina and Senator Charles Sumner of the Commonwealth of Massachusetts.

Congressman Brooks had taken offense to an anti slavery speech that Senator Sumner had given days earlier in which Sumner had made several violent sexual references to slavery, its supporters and South Carolina specifically. The speech was too much for Brooks. Congressman Brooks confronted Senator Sumner and proceeded to beat the living shit out of him with his metal-tipped cane. He beat Senator Sumner until he was a bloody, unconscious pulp. The Senator was beaten so badly that it took years for him to recover and he wouldn't fully resume his duties in the United States Senate until 1858. The outrage of this event would last well into the 1860s. Congressman Brooks would resign from the United States House of Representatives shortly after the fracas. He would be received in the South as a hero. Sumner would be martyred in the North and became a rallying cry for all things anti-slavery. A discussion renewed on the merits of the First Amendment to the United States and the issue of free speech. Additionally, Congressmen and Senators started to carry knives and guns on their person for protection. So it was this climate that Senator Crittenden and Congressman Corwin worked to try to avoid secession and bloodshed. It's easy to see why both efforts failed.

The amendments proposed by Senator Crittenden were:

1. Slavery would be prohibited in any territory of the United States "now held, or hereafter acquired," north of latitude 36 degrees, 30 minutes line. In territories south of this line,

slavery of the African race was "hereby recognized" and could not be interfered with by Congress. Furthermore, property in African slaves was to be "protected by all the departments of the territorial government during its continuance." States would be admitted to the Union from any territory with or without slavery as their constitutions provided.

2. Congress was forbidden to abolish slavery in places under its jurisdiction within a slave state such as a military post.

3. Congress could not abolish slavery in the District of Columbia so long as it existed in the adjoining states of Virginia and Maryland and without the consent of the District's inhabitants. Compensation would be given to owners who refused consent to abolition.

4. Congress could not prohibit or interfere with the interstate slave trade.

5. Congress would provide full compensation to owners of rescued fugitive slaves. Congress was empowered to sue the county in which obstruction to the fugitive slave laws took place to recover payment; the county, in turn, could sue "the wrong doers or rescuers" who prevented the return of the fugitive.

6. No future amendment of the Constitution could change these amendments or authorize or empower Congress to interfere with slavery within any slave state.

Collectively, these amendments split the country into half slave states, half free states. These amendments also, would have kept Black people slaves forever, with no recourse for relief from servitude. Thankfully, President-Elect Abraham Lincoln and Northern Republicans squashed all of this shit.

The Corwin was a toned down version of the Crittenden Compromise. The result would not have been much better for Blacks however. For Blacks it was trading bull shit for horse shit but the stench was still the same from a social repercussion point of view. Since the amendment would have "protected" states rights as it pertained to slavery, this combined with the already enacted Fugitive Slave Law of 1850 was the same thing Senator Crittenden was saying all along. If passed war would have been averted and the slavery would have lasted well into the Twentieth Century when the rise of the Industrial Revolution and economics of modernization would have taken hold. If we assume this paradox, what else would have not happened? Well, President Lincoln lives for one. Although still famous, not nearly the icon he is today. Andrew Johnson footnotes into history like most Vice Presidents of the United States. As I stated in Three Blind Mice, the Vice President of the United States is a dingle berry that hangs from a hair on the President's ass.

Ulysses S. Grant maybe becomes a General in the United States Army. Even this is doubtful for without a war to fight his fondness for the bottle would have undoubtedly ruined his career and reputation. Either way he never becomes President of the United States. In the short term there is no need to address Black citizenship, or the right to vote. Yes, Radical Republicans would continue to make a fuss, but the Corwin Amendment would render them as Paper Tigers. America's foreign policy would have turned isolationist as much of the country's business would have been concentrated on building a nation from the Atlantic Ocean to the Pacific Ocean and organizing the various Territories into States. This brings us to the cases of two other states. Because the Corwin Amendment protected state institutions from infringement by the United States Federal Government Utah makes a strong argument for the practice of polygamy. Additionally, the State of Oregon proudly upholds their state's Constitution of not allowing Blacks to live in the State.

So the side effect of the defeat of the Corwin Amendment is significant on many levels. It's amazing to think that this amendment only existed to appease the two percent of the South's population that actually owned slaves. Matter of fact, historians note that going to war and seceding from the Union was much less popular in non-slaving holding areas of the South than in those regions with large slave holdings. What is equally amazing is that the Corwin Amendment actually passed both the United States House of Representatives and the United States Senate. And it would be ratified by the state legislatures of Ohio, Maryland and Illinois. Stingingly, since its ratification has no sunset, it is still pending ratification. It was even proposed for a vote on the floor of the State of Texas House of Representatives in 1963 by then Dallas Republican Henry Stollenwerck (in a true example of how far America had not come). Had the Corwin Amendment become part of the United States Constitution it's conceivable that slavery would have lasted well into the Twentieth Century and America would have become a pariah in the worldwide community of nations.

It would have taken another amendment to repeal it and, such an undertaking would have been very hard to come by, especially in the state legislatures of the South. So who was Thomas Corwin? Born in Ohio, in addition to serving in the United States House of Representatives, he was an attorney, a member of the State of Ohio House of Representatives, a United States Senator, the fifteenth Governor of Ohio and the twentieth United States Secretary of the United States Treasury under President Millard Fillmore. His nickname was "The Wagon Boy." A moniker he earned by serving as a wagon boy in then General (and future President of the United States) William Henry Harrison's army during the War of 1812. He came from a family of politicians as his father served as Speaker of the House in the Ohio House of Representatives. Additionally, his cousin Moses Bledso Corwin served in the United States House of Representatives from Ohio during the Thirty-first and Thirty-third United State Congresses. It is interesting to note that in a bit of Nineteenth Century reality television, like family dysfunction, Moses was opposed by his own son, John Corwin, in the 1848 United States Congressional Elections.

John Corwin would lose that election and several others over the course of his career. However he would be elected to the State of Ohio Supreme Court. Thomas Corwin's nephew Franklin Corwin was also a politician. He would serve in the United States House of Representatives from the State of Illinois. Franklin also served in both houses of the Ohio General Assembly and served as the Speaker of the House of the Illinois House of Representatives. Another amendment still pending is the Child Labor Amendment.

Offered in April, 1924 by United States Congressman Israel Moor Foster of Ohio the text reads as such:

Section 1. The Congress shall have power to limit, regulate, and prohibit the labor of persons under eighteen years of age.

Section 2. The power of the several States is unimpaired by this article except that the operation of State laws shall be suspended to the extent necessary to give effect to legislation enacted by the Congress.

Basically, the Child Labor Amendment was originated because earlier legislative attempts by the United States Federal Government had failed. All over the world the issue of child manipulation is a constant societal struggle. No matter the political or economic structure of a given nation there is always some adult willing to fuck over a child or children as a means to an end. Be it sex, religion or work. American democracy and capitalism is no exception. Although improvements can still be made when it comes to child labor, the United States is well ahead the curve of many other nations. In some countries if you can walk, you can work. It's real fucked-up bullshit. All around the world, including the United States, agriculture is by far the number one employer of children to varying degrees. Current United States federal law says a child as young as twelve can work on a farm unlimited hours outside of school hours with parental permission. While I think most adult farmers exercise excellent judgment when it comes to their workforce, there are always a few bad apples in the bunch. What's scary is to think about some kid on a farm in one of America's agricultural hotbeds waking at the crack of dawn and breaking his fucking back before the school bus comes to pick him or her up, going to school all fucking day, coming home and immediately going back out into the field. Nothing wrong with learning a good work ethic at a young age. America's problem is this same child has to compete with another kid who gets a good nights' sleep, hot breakfast, participates in extra-curricular activities, finishes his or her homework, gets the mental nutrition of quality family time and goes to bed at a reasonable hour to get up and do it all over again. This "sociological inequality" is just how one kid grows up a fucking serial killer and the other ends up running a Fortune Five Hundred company. In the Twenty-first Century it's estimated that children between the ages of twelve and eighteen, some half a million children, pick over twenty five percent of all of America's produce. So think about that the next time you are at a steakhouse enjoying an iceberg lettuce wedge salad smothered in bleu cheese and bacon bits.

Or savoring a beefsteak tomato served with buffalo mozzarella and basil drizzled with extra virgin oil and balsamic vinegar. Or finishing off that New York strip with a fully loaded baked potato. Hey, I'm as guilty as every fucking body else. And I love that shit. It's just sad to know that there's a one in four chance some kid who should be doing his Civics homework about the Amendments to the United States Constitution labored over the overpriced shit on my plate. Other nations are more fucked up than the United States. In Africa fifty percent of children do some kind of shit work. And that doesn't include the boys forced to man an AK-47 and become child soldiers. The United Nations estimates over one hundred sixty eight million children between the ages of five and seventeen are working somewhere around the world. In Asia one quarter of the workforce is child labor. In China and India that's from a population of one billion in each country. That's a lot of exploitation. In Latin

America children make up seventeen percent of the workforce. To put this in perspective in the United States the number of children working is about one percent.

So it is this backdrop the Child Labor Amendment came into being. The direct event was the striking down as unconstitutional by the United States Supreme Court of two other pieces of legislation. The Keating-Owen Act of 1916 and the Child Labor Tax Law of 1919. Neither of these laws dealt upfront with the morality of child labor in the same way that the Child Labor Amendment would have. Instead, both laws simply "discouraged" child labor and the United States Supreme Court was absolutely right in opining them as unconstitutional. When the United States Supreme Court put a bullet in the Child Labor Tax Law Capitol Hill figured it was time for an amendment. This is the beauty of the amendment process. The only bodies involved are the Legislature Branch of the United States Government and the individual states themselves. The President of the United States has no say in its creation (although the modern Presidency and the power of the bully pulpit can certainly influence a populace) and once passed and ratified by the proper number of states the United States Supreme Court can't do shit about it. It's like the ultimate version of the show Survivor, Survivor's Tribal Council.

Two entities can get together (the state and Congress) and totally squeeze out the other two entities (the Executive and Judicial Branches). First, the Keating-Owen Act. Passed in 1916, the legislation prohibited the sale of goods made by children in interstate commerce. Supported by then President Woodrow Wilson, the United States Supreme Court said just because a product is made by a child it makes no sense that that same product can't be bought by anyone anywhere. The Act's authors were Ed Keating and Robert Latham Owen. Keating was a United States Representative from the state of Colorado. Owen was a United States Senator from the state of Oklahoma. Born in Kansas City, Kansas (commonly known as KCK), Keating was a newspaper man who first got into politics in the late 1890s. He was a son of Irish immigrants and the fact that he never finished high school may have contributed to his feelings on child labor. Keating's co-sponsor of the Child Labor Amendment was United States Senator Robert Latham Owen. Senator Owen was an active legislator who was also known for being one of the sponsors of the Federal Reserve Act of 1913. He even ran for President of the United States in 1919.

After the striking down of the Keating-Owen Act the United States Congress passed the Child Labor Tax Law in 1919. The law imposed a ten percent tax on any company that employed children. Again their hearts were in the right place but the United States Supreme Court saw things differently. The Court ruled that the imposition of a tax was actually a criminal penalty and thusly unconstitutional. The case was Bailey v. Drexel Furniture Co. Drexel Furniture was a North Carolina manufacturer who was assessed a tax levy per the Child Labor Tax Law. It was delivered by a Collector named J.W. Bailey working for the Bureau of Internal Revenue (the forerunner of the Internal Revenue Service). Drexel paid the fine but sued the government for a refund. Ironically, the Chief Justice of the United States Supreme Court at the time was none other than the former President of the United States William Howard Taft. His opinion stated that if left unabated the United States Congress can create any penalty it wanted and disguise it each time as a tax. This would make a great argument for the many opponents of Obamacare.

Probably one of the most influential figures who cast a very bright light on child labor and how fucked up it can be was the photographer Lewis Hines. Working with the National Child Labor Committee, in 1908 Hines started on a ten year journey of documenting, through photography, the ills of child labor. He was well known for his photographs of child laborers working for America's textile industry. After the failure of these two acts the United States Congress decided to pass the Child Labor Amendment. It was sponsored by Republican Congressman Israel Moore Foster. Foster represented the state of Ohio in the United States House of Representatives. Foster graduated from Ohio University and obtained a law degree from Ohio State University. He would also serve as the prosecuting attorney for Athens County, Ohio. The Child Labor Amendment would be ratified by twenty-eight states. With fifty states in the current Union it would take ratification of another ten states to become part of the United States Constitution. Ultimately the stock market crash of 1929 and the subsequent Great Depression would mitigate the issue of child labor. By this time adults were so desperate for work that even a child's wages would suffice for most adults who wanted to work.

Next up was the Equal Rights Amendment or commonly known as the ERA. Originally written and introduced to the United States Congress in 1923 it would not pass both houses of the United States Congress until 1972. Amazing, considering the turmoil of the Vietnam War, and every kind of protest you can think of. 1972 was the continuation of a fight that continues into the Twenty-first Century.

The text of the amendment:

Section 1. Equality of rights under the law shall not be denied or abridged by the United States or by any State on account of sex.

Section 2. The Congress shall have the power to enforce, by appropriate legislation, the provisions of this article.

Section 3. This amendment shall take effect two years after the date of ratification.

Equal rights for women in the United States started in the 1850s with the Women's Suffrage movement. Women like Elizabeth Cady Stanton, Lucy Stone, Susan B. Anthony, Sojourner Truth and others set the stage for what would become the Nineteenth Amendment to the United States Constitution. The Nineteenth Amendment will be discussed later in the book. It soon became clear that just getting the right to vote didn't end daily marginalization of women in the United States. As personalities go there were three driving forces behind the legislation. First there was Alice Paul who drafted the wording for the Equal Rights Amendment. She was a leading suffragist in the early 1900s. The other two were United States Senator Charles Curtis and United States Representative Daniel R. Anthony Jr. Congressman Anthony was quite sympathetic to the movement since his aunt was none other than Susan B. Anthony. Both the Senator and Congressman represented the state of Kansas and the Republican Party.

Born in Moorestown, New Jersey Alice Paul was not just a woman who was fed up with taking shit from men. She was turbo educated and very articulated. She received her undergraduate degree in Biology from Swarthmore College. Swarthmore College was an institution co-founded by her grandfather. That's a great way to ensure your kid gets into college no matter what. Just start one. Although, by all accounts Paul was a brilliant high school student and could have gone to any university she chose. Her credentials didn't stop there. She also earned postgraduate degrees in sociology and economics, a masters and doctorate respectively from the University of Pennsylvania of the Ivy League. She also earned a law degree from American University. So Dr. Paul knew her shit in other words. Dr. Paul learned the suffrage game during her time in the United Kingdom, where she also studied at the University of Birmingham. As in the United States, women in Great Britain were sick of taking shit from men as well. And the suffrage movement was well organized and efficient.

Paul would bring these methods back to the United States and start working on equal rights in the early 1900s. Way before Martin Luther King Jr. began his non-violence campaign in the name of civil rights in America Alice Paul was doing it in the early 1900s in the name of woman's rights. When we get to the chapter on the Nineteenth Amendment you will hear about her efforts and the way her group was treated by White men. She would eventually seek to add woman's rights language to the Civil Rights Act of 1964 (unsuccessfully) and finally see passage of the Equal Rights Amendment in both houses of the United States Congress in 1972. Charles Curtis was as diverse a politician as any in American history. He represented the state of Kansas in both the United States House of Representatives and the United States Senate. In the Senate he also served as Majority Leader and President Pro Tempore. Ultimately, he would serve as Vice President of the United States in

President Herbert Hoover's Administration. Uniquely, especially for the time, Charles Curtis' accomplishments were realized despite the fact that he was half Native American. This, in an era when racism in the United States was at its peak. He was born and raised on a Native American reservation in Topeka, Kansas in 1860 when Kansas was still a territory. He graduated from Topeka High School, went on to study law, was admitted to the bar in 1881 and eventually became Prosecuting Attorney for Shawnee County, Kansas. Along with Representative Daniel R. Anthony Jr. in 1923 he would first present the Equal Rights Amendment to Congress. The shit went nowhere however. His Native American background would greatly influence his backing of equal rights throughout his political career including when he became Vice President. Daniel R. Anthony Jr. was born in Leavenworth, Kansas to newspaper publisher and brother of Susan B. Anthony Daniel R. Anthony Sr. He would attend the University of Michigan and follow in his father's footsteps becoming Editor of the Leavenworth Times, to this day the oldest daily newspaper in the state of Kansas. His father, Daniel Sr. was a real piece of work. He, along with Susan was one of eight children born in Adams, Massachusetts. He was an abolitionist and went to Kansas to get into the popular sovereignty fight going on there in the 1850s. Daniel Sr. was also apt to find trouble on occasion. He once shot and killed a man who called him a coward.

He was once shot himself as well as stabbed by another man. Daniel Jr. would eventually make his way to the United States House of Representatives taking over the seat once held by Charles Curtis who moved over to the United States Senate. Between 1923 and 1972 the Equal Rights Amendment would take many twists and turns. Most of the back and forth were between differing factions of women themselves. Alice

Paul and the National Women's Party wanted outright gender equality. Other women's groups saw women as uniquely different from men and wanted to make sure those differences were recognized in the overall discussion of equality. There are similarities to the Civil Rights Movement of the 1960s. Malcolm X has one vision, which was hawkish, defiant and blunt. Martin Luther King Jr. had a vision that was dovish, guilt ridden and determined. Like the women's/feminist both sides had their place. The back and forth bickering kept the Equal Rights Amendment from ever making it to the floor of either side of the United States Congress for many years. However, it did get floor votes in the years 1946, 1950 and 1953.

The other problem with the legislation was a cleverly worded provision called the Hayden Rider. Introduced by United States Senator Carl Hayden in 1950 it read as follows:

"The provisions of this article shall not be construed to impair any rights, benefits, or exemptions now or hereafter conferred by law upon persons of the female sex."

Now I don't know what the fuck this means and I ain't gonna act like I do. What is fact is that proponents of the Amendment hated it and opponents of the Amendment didn't think it went far enough. Alice Paul and the National Women's Party decided the Amendment was better off dead than passing with the Hayden Rider. President Dwight D. Eisenhower was the first President of the United States to support the Amendment asking a Joint Session of Congress to pass it in 1958. The Equal Rights Amendment would be a part of the Republican platform every year until 1980. This is a stark contrast to today's argument that the

Republican Party is anti-woman. President John F. Kennedy supported the Amendment during the Election of 1960 but backed away after he won the election so not to piss off the labor unions that did not support it. Part of the Civil Rights Act of 1964 did include language regarding equal rights for women banning workplace discrimination on the basis of sex, but it was watered down protection at best. Finally in 1971 the United States House of Representatives passed the Equal Rights Amendment as presented by Representative Martha Griffiths of Michigan. The United States Senate would approve the House Joint Resolution in March, 1972. Having passed the United States House of Representatives and the United States Senate the Equal Rights Amendment moved to the ratification process by the individual states. It would need a minimum of thirty eight states to become part of the United States Constitution. The Equal Rights Amendment was unique in that part of the language included a seven year "sunset" on state ratification. Meaning that if the required number of state legislatures didn't pass the Equal Rights Amendment by March, 1979 the shit would die altogether. This was a great loophole for opponents of the measure.

It meant they would only have to stave it off for that seven year window which they effectively did. That fight wasn't easy either within the first year thirty states had ratified the Amendment. Getting those other eight ratification was a bitch though (no pun intended). During the six ensuing years only five more state legislatures would ratify the Amendment. So even in the Twenty First Century the United States of America has no constitutional guarantees for its women citizens. While America is quick to speak about woman's rights and shame other countries (especially the non-White nations), the failure to pass the Equal Rights Amendments exposes American hypocrisy and represents a failure of legislature leadership. It should be noted that seven individual states have passed their own version of an Equal Rights Amendments. They are:

Alaska

California

Colorado

Iowa

Maryland

Utah

Wyoming

So kudos to the above for accomplishing what the collective could not.

Chapter 4

᠖

State Legislatures: All Politics is Local

A crucial part of the Amendment process is ratification by a majority of the individual state legislatures. Today that number is thirty eight out of fifty states. Before we continue examining the twenty seven actual Amendments to the United States Constitution let's have a look at the state legislatures, who represents, who actually is in power and how they got there. To really understand one has to look at the structure of state government in the United States. And, like everything else in America it starts with money. Or, in this case the lack thereof. Most state legislators get paid very little and, in some cases what most of us would describe as a "pittance." More often than not the Congressman or Senator who is letting you down in Washington made his bones in a state legislative body first. Yes, there is the occasional war hero and feel good story candidate that gets elected but for the most part it's a very organized and deliberate process. And it's controlled by a few very powerful elite.

In my first book Three Blind Mice I mentioned how hard it is to become President of the United States and that if your filling your kid's head up with that bullshit you should just stop. Well the same thing applies if you think your kid is ever going to be part of a state's legislature. The system is already rigged. And it's built to stay that way. Why? Let's see. As I said when I opened up this chapter compensation for an individual tending to the states business pays shit money (unless you become a public servant for the state of California). Add to this the fact that there aren't that many slots to go around and you get a situation of the few representing the many. Often times this means minorities get squeezed out and have no say in their day to day lives. The breakdown of each state's legislative compensation (numbers are rounded):

Alabama – Ten thousand annually
Alaska – Fifty thousand annually
Arizona – Twenty four thousand annually
Arkansas – Fifteen thousand annually
California – Ninety thousand annually
Colorado – Thirty thousand annually
Connecticut – Twenty eight thousand annually
Delaware – Forty one thousand annually
Florida – Thirty thousand annually
Georgia – Seventeen thousand annually
Hawaii – Forty eight thousand annually
Idaho – Sixteen thousand annually
Illinois – Sixty seven thousand annually
Indiana – Twenty two thousand annually
Iowa – Twenty five thousand annually
Kansas – Eighty eight dollars per day
Kentucky – One hundred eighty six dollars per day
Louisiana – Fifteen thousand annually

Maine – Twenty three thousand annually

Maryland – Forty four thousand annually

Massachusetts – Fifty eight thousand annually

Michigan – Seventy two thousand annually

Minnesota – Thirty one thousand annually

Mississippi – Ten thousand annually

Missouri – Thirty six thousand annually

Montana – Eighty two dollars per day

Nebraska – Twelve thousand annually

Nevada – One hundred forty seven dollars per day

New Hampshire – One hundred dollars annually (two hundred dollars per two year term)

New Jersey – Forty nine thousand annually

New Mexico – State legislators get paid zero

New York – Eighty thousand annually

North Carolina – Fourteen thousand annually

North Dakota – One hundred forty eight dollars per day

Ohio – Sixty one thousand annually

Oklahoma – Thirty eight thousand annually

Oregon – Twenty two thousand annually

Pennsylvania – Seventy eight thousand annually

Rhode Island – Fifteen thousand annually

South Carolina – Ten thousand annually

South Dakota = Twelve thousand annually

Tennessee – Nineteen thousand annually

Texas – Seven thousand annually

Utah – One hundred seventeen dollars per day

Vermont – Six hundred thirty six dollars per week

Virginia – Eighteen thousand annually

Washington – Forty two thousand annually

West Virginia – Twenty thousand annually

Wisconsin – Fifty thousand annually

Wyoming – One hundred fifty dollars per day

So, what does the above all mean? It means on average an individual working as a public servant in a particular State's legislature is paid approximately twenty seven thousand dollars annually. Even that number is wildly skewed by the nine states who pay their legislators over fifty thousand dollars annually.

They are:

Alaska

California

Illinois

Massachusetts

Michigan

New York

Ohio

Pennsylvania

Wisconsin

The national average would put state legislative salaries just above the United States Federal Government's definition of poverty. In 2014 the United States Federal Government monetarily defined poverty as any family making just under twenty four thousand dollars annually. Yet, strangely there is never a news story about some legislator crying poor mouth about trying to make ends meet. So how can anyone afford to do such shit paying work? This is where the system is rigged to keep most Americans on the outside and marginalized by the few. At that kind of pay a position with such power can only be afforded by someone already well off. Think business owner, doctor, lawyer, etc. or a child of a professional. And none of this takes into account how much it cost to even mount an election campaign, no matter the level of office. Also, remember that these individuals assume office not only with their constituents in mind but, also with the interest of themselves and their friends in mind as well. Both the friends they have known all of their lives and the new ones they pick up along the way. This process can't be helped, it's human nature. Exploitation is inevitable. So "income inequality" also leads to "power inequality."

What is amazing (in a good way) about American politics is the fact that it's not more corrupt than it really is. This is an important fact to know as it relates to the United States Constitutional Amendment process. The average American could be getting fucked over a lot more than he or she already is. What's also compelling about your misrepresentation at the state level is that a disproportionate few represent a constituency way beyond an individual legislator's ability to effectively look out for their interests as a whole. The lone exception might be the legislature in the state of New Hampshire. Known as the New Hampshire General Court it has four hundred members in the General Court's New Hampshire House of Representatives. In the General Court's New Hampshire Senate there are twenty four members. How big (in terms of membership) is the New Hampshire General Court? Globally there are only three larger English speaking legislative bodies. They include the Parliament of the United Kingdom, the Parliament of India and the United States Congress. The New Hampshire General Court is the largest legislature in the United States by far. If, the representation to population was extrapolated on a national scale, the United States Congress would have over ninety nine thousand members.

These four hundred and twenty four individuals represent the interests of a one million three hundred thousand population. As outrageous as that sounds it's your best shot in America to actually think there is someone at the state level of politics looking after you. Before you pack your bags and start crossing state lines en masse think about this: Just don't plan on participating as a member of the Court. New Hampshire legislators are paid two hundred dollars for the TERM. That's one hundred dollars a year. Only those already well off could afford to work for such paltry pay. And New Hampshire has arguably (at least in theory) the fairest numerical political system in the nation. There are wider disparities in other states however. See below how few people represent the many. Then refer back to the salaries listed earlier in the chapter. This will give you an idea of how politically insignificant most Americans really are and why the same group of people stay in power from generation to generation. The "lack" of salary is the elite's political "sleight of hand" that has made politics a Blue Blood business in the United States of America. It's America's original lineage society, so to speak:

In the State of Alabama one hundred forty individuals represent four million eight hundred thousand citizens.

In the State of Alaska sixty individuals represent seven hundred thirty five thousand citizens.

In the State of Arizona ninety individuals represent six million six hundred thousand citizens.

In the State of Arkansas one hundred thirty five individuals represent three million citizens.

In the State of California one hundred twenty individuals represent THIRTY EIGHT MILLION citizens. This is my recommendation of a state to move to if you're seeking the most political irrelevancy you can find.

In the State of Colorado one hundred individuals represent five million (many pot smoking) citizens.

In the State of Connecticut one hundred eighty seven individuals represent three million five hundred thousand citizens.

In the State of Delaware sixty two individuals represent nine hundred and twenty five thousand citizens.

In the State of Florida one hundred sixty individuals represent nineteen million five hundred thousand citizens.

In the State of Georgia two hundred thirty six individuals represent ten million citizens.

In the State of Hawaii seventy six individuals represent one million four hundred thousand citizens.

In the State of Idaho one hundred five individuals represent one million six hundred thousand citizens.

In the State of Illinois one hundred seventy seven individuals represent twelve million eight hundred thousand citizens.

In the State of Indiana one hundred fifty individuals represent six million five hundred thousand citizens.

In the State of Iowa one hundred fifty individuals represent three million citizens.

In the State of Kansas one hundred sixty five individuals represent two million nine hundred thousand citizens.

In the Commonwealth of Kentucky one hundred thirty eight individuals represent four million four hundred thousand citizens.

In the State of Louisiana one hundred forty four individuals represent four million six hundred thousand citizens.

In the State of Maine one hundred eighty eight individuals represent one million three hundred thousand citizens.

In the State of Maryland one hundred eighty eight individuals represent six million citizens.

In the Commonwealth of Massachusetts two hundred individuals represent six million seven hundred thousand citizens.

In the State of Michigan one hundred forty eight individuals represent nine million nine hundred thousand citizens.

In the State of Minnesota two hundred one individuals represent five million four hundred thousand citizens.

In the State of Mississippi one hundred seventy four individuals represent three million citizens.

In the State Missouri one hundred ninety seven individuals represent six million citizens.

In the State of Montana one hundred fifty individuals represent one million citizens.

In the State of Nebraska forty nine individuals represent one million eight hundred thousand citizens. Even more unique to Nebraska is the fact that they are a unicameral law making body. Meaning instead of having a house of representatives and a senate, they have one nonpartisan chamber. Nebraska also has the smallest of any state legislature in America. So the downside for Nebraskans is that their representation is shitty in a lot of ways. The upside is it's a lot easier for a single group of forty nine people to get things done than it is for some other states legislatures. So pick your poison.

In the State of Nevada sixty three individuals represent two million seven hundred thousand citizens.

In the State of New Hampshire four hundred twenty four individuals represent one million three hundred thousand citizens.

In the State of New Jersey one hundred twenty individuals represent eight million nine hundred thousand citizens.

In the State of New Mexico one hundred twelve individuals represent two million citizens.

In the State of New York two hundred twelve individuals represent nineteen million six hundred thousand citizens.

In the State of North Dakota one hundred forty one individuals represent seven hundred twenty thousand citizens.

In the State of North Carolina one hundred seventy individuals represent nine million eight hundred thousand citizens.

In the State of Ohio one hundred thirty two individuals represent eleven million five hundred thousand citizens

In the State of Oklahoma one hundred forty nine individuals represent three million eight hundred thousand citizens.

In the State of Oregon ninety individuals represent three million nine hundred thousand citizens.

In the Commonwealth of Pennsylvania two hundred fifty three individuals represent twelve million seven hundred thousand citizens.

In the State of Rhode Island and Providence Plantations (its official name) one hundred thirteen individuals represent one million citizens.

In the State of South Carolina one hundred seventy individuals represent four million seven hundred thousand citizens.

In the State of South Dakota one hundred five individuals represent eight hundred forty four thousand citizens.

In the State of Tennessee one hundred thirty two individuals represent six million five hundred thousand citizens.

In the State of Texas one hundred eighty one individuals represent twenty six million five hundred thousand citizens.

In the State of Utah one hundred four individuals represent two million nine hundred thousand citizens.

In the State of Vermont one hundred eighty individuals represent six hundred twenty six thousand citizens.

In the Commonwealth of Virginia one hundred forty individuals represent eight million two hundred thousand citizens.

In the State of Washington one hundred forty seven individuals represent seven million citizens.

In the State of West Virginia one hundred thirty four individuals represent one million eight hundred thousand citizens.

In the State of Wisconsin one hundred thirty two individuals represent five million seven hundred thousand citizens.

And in the State of Wyoming ninety individuals represent five hundred eighty two thousand citizens.

In Twenty First Century America it takes thirty eight of the fifty states to ratify an Amendment to the United States Constitution. With the current political system in place it would seem almost an impossibility to get an Amendment passed even if there was the political will. On the other hand states rights and the power therein has never been stronger.

Chapter 5

❧

The Twenty Seven Amendments on the Books, The Bill of Rights, The First Ten Amendments to the United States Constitution

Starting with the Bill of Rights, adopted in 1792 to the Twenty Seventh Amendment adopted in 1992, there are currently twenty seven Amendments to the United States Constitution that are currently law. We will look at each one, how they came about and what they mean to all Americans in present day. What were some of the outside influences that affected the codified Amendments? Well the United States Constitution for one. Another was the argument between the Federalists and the Anti-Federalists. One unique influence on the Amendments to the United States Constitution was specifically the Federalist Papers and more specifically the essay that became Federalist Number Eighty Four. Written by Alexander Hamilton, a Founding Father of the United States and James Madison, fourth President of the United States, respectively the writings continue to hover over the United States Constitution to this day. These two teamed up with John Jay, the first Chief Justice of the United States Supreme Court and third author of the Federalist Papers, to help make the United States Constitution what it is. Let's start with the United States Constitution. I'm not going into the specifics of each article, there's been plenty written on the topic so simply go read about it. However, know this; if you are an American citizen it is part of your daily life each and every day. From when you wake up in the morning and brush your teeth to commuting to work to how you raise your children to taking a good shit.

The United States Constitution is with you all the way. The document sets guidelines for how you seek and maintain food, clothing and shelter. How you conduct commerce. The document also protects you from the crazy assholes of the rest of the world, both historically and present day. These include such fuck ups as Hitler, Stalin, Saddam Hussein and various terrorists of all sorts. The Constitution's checks and balances make sure no one person can ever fuck you over. So, overall it's a helluva thing. What guides it all is how humans interpret, initiate and enforce the tome. While I think the Founding Fathers felt good about the finished product they also knew they needed a back door so future generations could add on to whatever they may have left out. Thusly the Amendments to the United States Constitution. On the whole, the United States Constitution and its subsequent Amendments is THE LAW and nobody can fuck with it.

The Federalist Papers were to the United States Constitution what Don King was to boxing promotion. The papers were the hype machine to get everyone on board with this new document. A total of eighty five Papers were written in all. As mentioned earlier they were all written by Alexander Hamilton, James Madison and John Jay. Hamilton wrote the most by far having penned fifty one of them. To keep the boxing analogy going every Ali needs a Frazier. While the Federalists argued for a strong central government the Anti Federalists argued for strong state government. It's ironic that this argument would lead to the American Civil War and continue today in a new iteration between Democrats and Republicans. Anyway, as it relates to the Amendment to the United States Constitution Federalist Number Eighty Four, written by James Madison, actually argues that the Bill of Rights was an unnecessary waste of legal pronouncements. Madison argued that the Bill of Rights were not necessary because, in effect these Amendments were implied. In many ways he felt that the United States Congress and the States were amending the United States Constitution just because it could.

So let's look at the Amendments and why they were deemed relevant.

The First Ten Amendments to the United States Constitution: The United States Bill of Rights

It's ironic that James Madison would oppose the Bill of Rights as he would be the one who would propose them. This was in part to assuage the Anti Federalists who demanded more guarantees than were given in the United States Constitution. Initially the United States Bill of Rights was to be made up of twelve Amendments to the United States Constitution. It's amazing that they got any of them passed at all. There were many people that felt amending the United States Constitution so soon after its adoption would show the new government to be weak and indecisive. But Madison pressed on. He would go on to become a force in early American politics and leave a clear mark on the history of the United States ultimately becoming the Fourth President of the United States.

His story goes back much farther than that however. In addition to being known as the Father of the Constitution and the Father of the Bill of Rights he publicly served in several other capacities. James Madison was born in Orange County in the Commonwealth of Virginia. This is the same county where future President and hero of the Mexican American War Zachary Taylor was born as well. Madison's father, James Madison Sr. was a plantation/slave owner who made his money in tobacco. He served as a Colonel during the American Revolutionary War. Like all slave owning families in the colonial South, James Madison Jr. grew up a child of the elite. So they never worried about the ends meeting. Both the Madisons and the ends did just fine. Madison's marriage to Dolly Payne caused a bit of a stir (at least on her side of things) as Dolly was a widow and a Quaker and as such, forbidden to marry a non-Quaker. Forbidden for the Quaker thing not the widow thing. But since the heart wants what the heart wants they got married anyway and the Quakers promptly unfriended Dolly by expelling her from the church. She didn't give a fuck though. As far as she was concerned she found her new man and that was that. Dolly was with James through every public role he would serve which, outside of President of the United States included:

Delegate in the Virginia State Legislature
Delegate to the Congress of the Confederation
Member of the United States House of Representatives from
the Commonwealth of Virginia
Fifth United States Secretary of State
The First Amendment to the United States Constitution

The text reads as such:

Congress shall make no law respecting an establishment of religion, or prohibiting the free exercise thereof; or abridging the freedom of speech, or of the press; or the right of the people peaceably to assemble, and to petition the Government for a redress of grievances.

The First Amendment to the United States Constitution spells out five different things the United States Government CAN'T do (no matter who it pisses off) all in one sentence. The Government can't mandate you to mindlessly follow a supreme being of their choice. Furthermore, whatever Supreme Being you do choose to follow is none of their fucking business. This is important because ninety percent of the world believes in some kind of god.

The whole idea of freedom of religion in America goes back to the Roman Catholic Church, the Holy Roman Empire, the Church of England and Henry VIII's dick. Let me explain. In the early Sixteenth Century Catholicism was THE religion in Old World Europe. However, its grip on mind control through religion was chafing. Guys like Martin Luther and John Calvin were stirring up the pot and King Henry VIII was a young monarch who had fucking on his mind much more than representing his loyal subjects. He wasn't the first and wouldn't be the last; however his quest for pussy would change the world. When he got sick of fucking his wife, Catherin of Aragon, he found a feisty little thing named Anne Boleyn. She was cute, sexy and sharp at the mouth. Henry's quest for Anne's honey pot would lead to England's break from the Catholic Church, the establishment of the Church of England (which all subject HAD to submit to) and energize the Counter Reformation Movement. Oh, and also lead to Anne getting her fucking head cut off when he got sick of fucking her as a side note. What was the religion of the land would change several times depending on the reigning monarch of the day.

Henry's daughter Mary (known as Bloody Mary) would reinstall Catholicism and Elizabeth (known as the Virgin Queen) would turn around and reinstall the Church of England. Eventually the Church of England would prevail. Either way the new United States of America was not putting up with that bullshit and the first part of the one sentence First Amendment becomes the opening salvo to the Bill of Rights. And it all harkens back to King Henry VIII's one eyed snake so I says! So whether your Jewish, Protestant, Lutheran, Methodist, Baptist, Mormon, Islamic, Episcopalian, Jehovah's Witness, Catholic, Calvinist or a Five Percenter, in the United States of America you can get your pray on. The second part guarantees the freedom of speech. This means, in the macro, you can say whatever the fuck you want whenever the fuck you feel like it. In practice it means, to this day, if a motherfucker is a motherfucker and you know he or she is a motherfucker you can call him a motherfucker. He or she may not like knowing that fact but they reserve the right to respond in kind and say "so is your mother!" Try saying that shit to a Chinese politician, or some Russian official working out of the Kremlin or any fucking African despot (take your pick).

You also better watch what you say in the many of the theocracies of the Arab world as well. And North Korea? Shiiit! Your family would be like "what happened to so and so?" "Oh that motherfucker didn't know how to shut up and he won't be joining us for dinner ever again." Must've thought he was in America. Dumbass. This is why groups like the KKK, the Neo Nazis and Skinheads can spout their bullshit without recourse. The same goes for American militia groups, Black shakedown artists who feed off of White guilt and ethically challenged politicians who garner votes through scare tactics. The beauty of the First Amendment protects all of these motherfuckers. While protecting these individuals freedom of speech the First Amendment also encourages debate during the political process. And debate is the real check and balance of America as a Republic. It is sad to note that in the Twenty First Century two party political system this ability to debate often breakdowns and leads to legislative stagnation. The third part of the First Amendment to the United States Constitution guarantees freedom of the press. This doesn't mean that governments at all levels don't try to keep shit from getting out.

It does, however, mean that if some nosy motherfucker (like a print or broadcast journalist) gets ahold of some juicy information they can tell every fucking body and live to do the shit again. Freedom of the press allows for other mundane tidbits to be shared as well. Like a weather forecaster fucking up the ten day forecast, or some dickhead to go on television and push a shitty book or movie, to some news anchor telling you about some asshole who got shot at the club over the weekend. But the best part of freedom of the press is exposing the hypocrisy of the government and politicians and their way too much crookedness. Freedom of the press also protects whistle blowers. Unless, of course, you blow the whistle on some government agency that doesn't want you to know their listening to you have phone sex. Some perverted computer nerd getting his jollies at your expense has definitely got to be kept a secret! Historically, freedom of the press has played a significant role in America's past. Some examples:

Exposing the evils of slavery in the Nineteenth Century prior to the Civil War. The corrupt administrations of Presidents Ulysses S. Grant and Warren G. Harding. The scandals of Watergate, Iran-Contra and Monica Lewinsky. And don't forget about the press skewering wannabee

Presidents Gary Hart and John Edwards for getting their freak on. In the 1988 Presidential Election George H. W. Bush used the press to make Willie Horton almost seem like Michael Dukakis' running mate and as a result Bush was sworn into the Office of President of the United States a few months shy of two hundred years after George Washington was sworn in as America's first President. Freedom of the press goes the other way too. Every President since George Washington has used the press to get the word out about his agenda. President James Madison used the press to rally support in the fight against the British during the War of 1812. President Andrew Jackson did it during his fight over the Second Bank of the United States and his expulsion of Native Americans that would lead to the Trail of Tears. President James K. Polk did the same prior to the Mexican American War. President Lincoln mastered using the press during the American Civil War. President William McKinley used the press to go to war with Spain.

President Theodore Roosevelt would use the press three ways. To trust bust the oligarchs of the early Twentieth Century, get the Panama Canal built and establish a national consciousness about America's national parks. President Woodrow Wilson would rally the United States to get into the fight in the latter half of World War One (although he would fail to use the press effectively in his efforts to establish the League of Nations). President Franklin Roosevelt was probably the master First Press Manipulator-in-Chief. His list of effective press use included pushing through the New Deal to getting America involved in World War Two (especially the justification of fighting the European portion of the war) to getting elected four times despite being a cripple. Matter of fact the only thing he didn't get the press to help him do was stack the United States Supreme Court. He was trying to get a little Executive Branch power greedy on that shit, however. President John F. Kennedy master-fully used the press during the Cuban Missile Crisis and jump starting NASA's Manned Moon missions.

Although President Lyndon B. Johnson got his ass handed to him on the Vietnam War by the press, however, he was adept at using the press on the issues of Civil Rights, the War on Poverty and the Great Society. President Ronald Reagan used the press to build a six hundred ship navy and win the Cold War. President George W. Bush used the press to sleight-of-hand the nation into war with Iraq. Finally President Barack Obama bully pulpited the press into supporting Obamacare. In all cases the press remains free and a vital of America's freedom process. Again, don't try any of this shit in the countries mentioned earlier in this chapter. The fourth piece of the First Amendment to the United States Constitution is the freedom to assemble. This part of the First Amendment has its genesis from the British reaction to the Boston Tea Party and the so called Intolerable Acts. Basically the British said to the Colonials "you know how serious we take out tea and if you're going to get together in gangs and fuck our shit up we'll just outlaw getting together to fuck shit up!" On the surface this sounds reasonable, how-ever, like with any law what makes it good or bad is person in charge of interpretation and application of the law. It's the standard "give a person an inch and they'll take a mile" idiom.

In this case the British decided to outlaw assembly altogether, peace-ful or otherwise. So the First Amendment makes sure if you want to get a group together and bitch about something, help yourself. Just remem-ber, be peaceful. Of course it doesn't always work out that way. When President Rutherford B. Hayes swapped Electoral College votes for an end to Reconstruction the southern states promptly made it hard as hell for Black folks to get together in any fashion. Suffragist Alice Paul got the shit kicked out of her assembling peacefully in her quest for women's rights. Martin Luther King Jr. gave his life for assembling peacefully in his efforts to make America live by its own heralded words. America's labor unions went to hell and back assembling peacefully while fighting for fair wages and better working conditions. Even today it doesn't stop the United States Government from trying to fuck with your right to peacefully assemble. In March of 2012 President Obama signed the Federal Restricted Buildings and Grounds Improvement Act or colloquially known as the Trespass Bill. It basically you CANNOT exercise your constitutional right to peacefully assemble if there is an event when an attendee requires United States Secret Service protection.

This means that you and your boys can't hangout if there is someone in the vicinity so powerful that the Secret Service has to be present to make sure they don't get shot. Yes, that is a federal fucking crime. The problem with this is the First Amendment and the whole United States Constitution for that matter says nothing about powerful people being the exception to the rule when it comes to assembling peacefully. The United States Government seems to be saying they don't want the fleas that come with this Constitutional dog. The last part of the First Amendment to the Constitution provides for the right to petition for redress of grievances. That's politically structured language for if the United States Government does something you think is fucked up (like listening in on your phone calls or reading your emails) you can ask for an answer as to why that shit is necessary. Ironically, this fifth guarantee in the First Amendment has taken a back seat to the other four and it's quite puzzling as to why. It basically says if the government is fucking over the people you can actually do something about it. Not like that asshole who tows your car and then holds it ransom till you fork over your next two house payments to get it back. The right to petition was first presented in exercise in the 1830s regarding slavery.

The Second Amendment to the United States Constitution

The Second Amendment to the United States Constitution is one of the most debated of all of the Amendments right up to present day America. The central question centers itself around the text itself. Which reads:

A well regulated militia being necessary to the security of a free state, the right of the people to keep and bear arms shall not be infringed.

This is fairly straightforward conceptually and then, not so straight at the same time. Words like "militia" and "people" make reference to a collective. The other question has always been does an individual have the right him or herself? I think the effects of British imperialism in application (meaning armed imperialism) greatly influenced America's right to bear arms. So the idea of protecting oneself from the crazies has been around for a long time. Regardless who gets defined as crazy. Historically, James Madison brought the language to the floor of the United States House of Representatives in June, 1789. It basically said you can own a gun to defend yourself. Interestingly it also included a conscientious objector provision. It said it a person is "religiously scrupulous" he can't be compelled to render military service. It was the ultimate "I'm a pussy get out of jail free" card. If your God told you that fighting was a bad thing all you would have to do was speak up.

Eventually, this clause would get thrown out with the baby water by the time it was forwarded to the United States Senate in August, 1789.

After chopping it up and sending it back to the United States House of Representatives it was ratified by the States on December 15, 1789 (whose two hundred twenty fifth anniversary was celebrated in 2014) was ratified as part of the Bill of Rights. So, in fewer six months the Legislative Branch of the United Government, in conjunction with the States themselves accomplished one of Democracy's greatest rule of law processes known to man. Very impressive, to say the least. Especially considering the fact that the conversations in both, the United States House of Representatives and the United States Senate got down to commas, individual words and placement of periods. Think about that and ask yourself could that ever happen (the passing of not one, but ten Amendments to the United States Constitution) in today's United States Government? And if you said "yes" your one of the most delusional motherfuckas paying taxes. Yes, I know all the arguments about there were fewer states, smaller population and a drastically smaller United States Government budget. They don't hold water because these men, as public servants, experienced the clash of purpose of cause, immediacy, and resolve. Of those three traits, today, one can argue there is an incredible lack of resolve in the political process of the United States. Over time the United States Supreme has used the Second Amendment to the United States Constitution in cases that have further defined or justify its relevance. In the Dred Scott decision the Second Amendment to the United States Constitution was cited to justify one of the overriding emotions the question of "are Blacks citizens?" United States Supreme Court Chief Justice Roger Taney was greatly influenced by the default that the United States Supreme Court ruled that, if Blacks were, in fact, citizens, then by definition they would have the privilege of exercising their Second Amendment rights. The idea of free Black people (and note that the Second Amendment to the United States Constitution does not stipulate gender in its text) walking around exercising the Second Amendment right scared the shit out of the White people of the day. There is no doubt that the United States Supreme didn't take long to figure out that when Black folks get around to mixing their Second Amendment rights with their First Amendment rights (especially the right to peacefully assemble) ruling that Blacks were not citizens of the United States was a no-fucking-brainer!

The Fourteenth Amendment to the United States Constitution (which we will talk about later) made all of this a moot point. Image how history would have changed from the mid 1860s and the passage of the Fourteenth Amendment, to the Twenty First Century if, American minorities had exercised their Second Amendment rights with the same enthusiasm as their European American counterparts? How does that change history and justice in America? I don't know the answer so help yourself to whatever you come with. At the end of the day, the Second Amendment killed any chance of Blacks getting citizenship via the Dred Scott decision. While not being a part of the Amendment process the United States Supreme Court does play a role in interpreting what the Amendments mean in application. Outside of defining the Fourteenth Amendment to every iteration known to man, the Second Amendment also gets a lot of play in the highest court of the Land. Specifically when it comes to the question of gun rights as it pertains to "militia" and "individual" ownership. The path to the Court settling the question of an individual's right to bear arms was finalized in the 2008 case District of Columbia v Heller. Some background:

Dick Heller was a police officer for the District of Columbia. While he could carry a firearm when he worked he was not allowed to possess one in his home since it was against District of Columbia law. He lived in South East D.C. Now, if you're familiar with Washington, D.C., while the White House and Capitol sit majestically with their manicured lawns and regal appearance, a mile away the reality of South East D.C. couldn't be more different. Let's just say it's the difference between law and lawlessness. So Heller was perfect as the face of a lawsuit challenging the District of Columbia law. Anyway, after winding its way through the lower court system the Supreme Court decided to address one simple question: Does the D.C law violate the Second Amendment right of an individual to be "strapped" in the privacy of his own home? The Court determined that the answer to that question was "yes." So the United States Supreme Court says you can you own a gun, it can be loaded and you can defend yourself from that fool that wants to disrupt your shit. And it doesn't matter if your part of a militia or not. This is a good thing because besides having a great basis of law America also had a ton of crazy motherfuckers who deserve a bullet in their ass.

Historically, this recognition of an individual's right to bear arms was not always recognized. For most of its history the Second Amendment was interpreted to mean that the States had a right gather up a militia and arm them when need be. Then it got watered down to if an individual was part of a militia, part time or otherwise, he or she (most often this meant "he" and White) then that individual could have and carry a gun. It was only after that bullshit didn't work that they said, "Ok, fuck it. Everyone can carry." However, today each State has a unique way of what they make you go through to get permission to carry. As you will read, in most states, there is some kind of "castle doctrine." Meaning if someone breaks into your house you should feel free to blast his or her ass and not fear retribution by law enforcement. By State (and I am factually generalizing):

Alabama:

The State of Alabama pretty much doesn't give a fuck whether you carry a gun or not. You don't need a permit, you don't need to register and you don't need a license. Have fun.

Alaska:

To be so far apart from each other they pretty much have the same laws as Alabama. One difference is that you can carry a firearm without a permit.

Arizona:

Welcome to the Wild West. You can pack heat with almost no restrictions. You don't need a permit, you can openly carry and, interestingly there are no magazine capacity requirements. Meaning you can tote around a gun that (paraphrasing Samuel L. Jackson's character in Jackie Brown) "if you need enough ammunition to kill every motherfucka in the room?" You can do it in Arizona.

Arkansas:

In the great state of Arkansas you don't need a permit, you don't need to register your weapon and you don't need a license. And help yourself to carrying a weapon, openly or concealed. As for magazine assault weapon restrictions? Nope. Have at it.

California

Now, in California they put you through a lot of shit to exercise your right to bear arms. In some form you have to have a permit, be registered and there are waiting periods on purchases. Licensing is taken care of via the requirement of being issued a weapons safety certificate. As for assault weapons and magazine capacity laws? You fucking right, they are in force and enforced. Much of California's current gun law legislation can be traced back to the 1960s and the Black Panther Party. Started in Oakland in 1966 the Black Panther Party was one of the early Black organizations of the day that confidently exercised their Second Amendment right to bear arms and their First Amendment right to peacefully assembly at the same time. While effective in practice the Black Panthers were, at times a bit overzealous and this drew the attention of law enforcement. Bringing loaded weapons to the steps of the state capitol in Sacramento was the straw that broke the camel's back. That was May, 1967. The site of Black men locked, loaded and unafraid was the impetus for California's gun laws as they exist today. California would be an example followed by many other states who had the same fear of their minority citizens exercising their right to bear arms.

Colorado:

Like many Western states not named California, Colorado allows its citizens a lot of space regarding gun ownership. No need for a permit, registration or license. However, in light of more than one mass shooting in the state the Colorado Legislature has amended some of it laws. If you want an assault weapon, get one but there are restrictions on magazine capacity.

Delaware:

The First State allows you to own a firearm without permit, license or registration. There is no assault weapon law or restriction on magazine capacity. If you've ever been to the DelMarVa Peninsula it's easy to understand why gun rights are so open for a state that resides in one of the nation's most populated areas.

Florida:

In Florida gun rights are also very important and the "individual" part of the Second Amendment's right to bear arms is tantamount. It is of note that if a law enforcement officer pulls you over and asks if you are carrying a weapon you don't' have to tell him shit. You have no "duty to inform." And, of course, you can definitely defend yourself if someone is threatening you no matter you are via "Stand Your Ground" legislation.

Georgia:

In Georgia, it's "Guns? Yes please!" Period.

Hawaii:

If you want to be almost completely relieved of your Second Amendment rights, Hawaii is the place for you. Simply put, if you want to possess a weapon you have to get a permit. And obtaining the permit is like the "N" and the "R" of New York City Subway fame. It's the "never" and the "rarely." But the sunsets and the surfing are great. "Mahalo."

Idaho:

In the State of Idaho the Second Amendment to the United States Constitution "is" the first amendment! You can arm yourself like you work for Nick Fury as long as you openly carry. So, feel free to go on down to Wal-Mart purchase your weapon, ammunition and holster and have at it.

Illinois:

In Chicago? Forget it. As for the rest of the state be prepared to get a register, license and permit in one form or another.

Indiana:

If you don't want the hassle of Illinois head east a little ways and get your Second Amendment on in Indiana. Outside of getting a permit and license to carry a pistol you can openly carry pretty much any kind of firearm your please. And you don't have to inform law enforcement if you are stopped.

Iowa:

The State of Iowa issues permits to carry "weapons" (concealed or otherwise). That means you can carry not only firearms, but whatever else you want scare a motherfucker with.

Kansas:

The State of Kansas makes it so easy to own a firearm they damn near issue you one along with a birth certificate when you're born. There are no permits or registration. No laws regarding assault weapons and you can open carry with a permit or registration.

Kentucky:

The Commonwealth of Kentucky is much like Kansas. The lone exception is that a license is issued to carry a concealed handgun.

Louisiana:

The State of Louisiana welcomes you to exercise your Second Amendment rights. It's not very hard at all. Which begs the question why so many people they have to own a gun illegally?

Maine:

The State of Maine is arguably the most "eastern, "Western-like" when it comes to your right to bear arms. And they are very quiet about it as well. Outside of a permit to carry a concealed handgun buy your gun today. And don't worry about any restriction as it pertains to assault weapons or magazine capacity.

Maryland:

The State of Maryland is almost the polar opposite to Maine in that you better be ready to give up an administrative kidney to own a gun. If it wasn't for Western Maryland and the residents of the Maryland portion of the DelMarVa Peninsula, you probably couldn't own a slingshot.

Massachusetts:

For a place where the very ideas of democracy were grown and fermented the Commonwealth of Massachusetts is nowhere to have a gun. There is some form of permit, license and/or registration throughout the state at all levels of government. And gun ownership is generally discouraged. As for assault weapons and restrictions on magazine capacities? Don't even think about it.

Michigan:

Michigan's gun laws are somewhere in the middle. They don't make it easy to bear arms, but, then again, they don't make it that hard either. Which makes you ask, as in the case of Louisiana, why are there so many illegal guns in its major cities? Although there are processes for permits, registrations and licensing, Michigan is a "shall issue" state when it comes to issuing these permits. Which means "you ask, you get."

Minnesota:

In the State of Minnesota, while they have restrictions as to assault weapons and magazine capacities your right (and under what circumstances) to bear arms hinges on one thing: Having a permit. That is specifically to carry, which allows the permit to purchase. The State holds those permits tight like a vice on your nuts. Minnesota also gives wide latitude to local authorities in creating their own laws.

Mississippi:

In the State of Mississippi the big deal with their firearm legislation is in the permits. The State has forty five days to issue a permit and it's good for five years. However, openly carrying a handgun is permitted in most cases without permit. Also, local governments cannot restrict a citizen's right to bear arms but can regulate conditions which those firearms may be discharged.

Missouri:

Like their liquor laws the Show Me State loves their guns too. In Missouri gun ownership and access to alcohol is a statewide Happy Meal. If that is your thing then this is where you need to live. Local governments may restrict openly carrying a firearm but for the most part your right to bear arms is upheld nicely.

Montana:

With its wide open space the citizen's of Montana enjoy great latitude in gun ownership. Open carry, concealed carry, assault weapons are all good to go. Exceptions being city or town limits and logging camps. Don't' worry about registration, permits or licenses. They don't' give a fuck.

Nebraska:

The Cornhusker State requires paperwork to be filed if you want to carry or purchase a gun. Registration of all handguns is required in the city of Omaha. So it is very easy to own a gun in the state.

Nevada:

Right to bear arms? You bet (pun intended)! Don't have a gun in Vegas, everywhere else, help yourself.

New Hampshire:

In the State of New Hampshire outside of not being able to carry a loaded gun in your car your right to bear arms is protected. As a citizen your access to a firearm is real easy. Notable given the fact most states in the Northeast United States crawl up your ass with a fucking microscope if you want to own a gun.

You need no permit to purchase, no registration is required licensing is under "shall issue" conditions. Meaning if you apply, you get.

New Jersey:

Speaking of states that crawl up your fucking ass with a microscope to own a gun; the State of New Jersey would be it. Part of this is due to the fact that New Jersey is the nation's most dense state in terms of population. That means there are a lot of people crammed in a small space. You gotta get a permit to purchase, you gotta be registered and your firearm must be registered. If you want to carry a handgun, forget it. The State's gun laws are constructed in such a way that New Jersey is "no issue" state. So this is where you want to live if you want to totally abandon your Second Amendment rights.

New Mexico:
The Land of Enchantment State is just the opposite of New Jersey. Outside of taking a gun safety course help yourself. The only other difference is that property owners can prohibit firearms when on their premises. Long guns, assault weapons and no magazine capacity are all allowed.

New York:
The Empire State is a lot like New Jersey. Leave your gun rights at the door. You can own a shotgun or rifle, but you better plan on using it. And if you live in New York City don't even think about it.

North Carolina:
The State of North Carolina is a defined gun state. It's even against the law for a government entity to make a law requiring registration. Refreshing. So, in the Tobacco State, smoke em' if ya got em' and get your gun on.

North Dakota:
In America's newest oil state your right to bear arms is a welcome thing. The only provision is that if you want to open carry a handgun it has to be during daylight hours and it unloaded and visible.

Ohio:
The State of Ohio protects your right to bear arms for the most part. You have to have training to carry a weapon but that's pretty much it. The city of Cleveland is the exception. Don't even think about it.

Oklahoma:

In Oklahoma there is no waiting period to purchase firearms. Concealed carry of loaded handguns is permitted. You do need a license to open carry a handgun.

Oregon:

The State of Oregon does little to impede your right to carry. The Oregon State Police does keep records of the sale of guns in the state. What is unusual about Oregon's guns statutes is that citizens can open carry not only handguns but long guns as well. Like most states major municipalities have their own restrictions. Which means no guns.

Pennsylvania:

The Commonwealth of Pennsylvania has a distinct right to bear arms as part of its constitution going back to 1790. Pennsylvania is a "shall issue" state.

Like other states major cities are, for the most part, gun free. In this case, Philadelphia. Everywhere else, open carry is "help yourself." The Commonwealth has a Castle law. Meaning if someone breaks into your home you can blast his ass to smithereens.

Rhode Island:

The State of Rhode Island says you have to take a training course to carry a gun. As for permits, local authorities operate a "shall issue" policy, but state authorities have a "may issue" policy in place. And since most local municipalities defer to the state attorney general Rhode Island is a no gun state unless you were are a retired police officer or something like that.

South Carolina:

The State of South Carolina is a gun state. If you want to carry a gun there are almost no restrictions. Assault weapons are allowed and there are no magazine capacity restrictions.

South Dakota:

The same goes for citizens in the State of South Dakota. As long as the weapon is visible you are free to open a gun.

Tennessee:

The State of Tennessee requires a permit to carry a handgun. Like a lot of states there is no requirement to retreat if you feel threatened. So, if you have to, put that motherfucker down.

Texas:

In the State of Texas you need a permit to carry however, for the most part, you rights to carry are well protected. Local governments can add other restrictions and they do.

Utah:

The Mormon State makes a distinction between carrying a loaded gun and an unloaded gun. You need a permit to carry a loaded gun but unloaded guns are fair game. In the State of Utah you can defend yourself if you feel threatened.

Vermont:

The State of Vermont is the "wow" state when it comes to gun ownership. This dates back to 1777 when Vermont was an independent republic and not part of the United States or a British colony. Simply put,

Vermont has almost no gun laws. If you're a citizen or visitor you can carry, openly or concealed, a firearm. Feel free to walk around with a rifle, shotgun, 44 magnum, 9mm or whatever you want. Silencers and other kinds of suppressors are prohibited but that's the case everywhere. In the Second Amendment advocate community the term "Vermont carry" is jargon for "fuck yeah I got a gun."

Virginia:

The Commonwealth of Virginia is a "shall issue" when it comes to permits. There are restrictions where assault weapons are concerned. There are also restrictions to gun ownership in the populated areas of Northern Virginia and areas around the Washington, D.C. metropolitan footprint. You are required to register automatic weapons with state law enforcement and proof of age and citizenship is required to purchase assault weapons. Openly carrying a firearm is generally allowed. If you are driving you have to put it "away." In the glove compartment, trunk or other item carrying space in the vehicle.

Washington:

The State of Washington requires gun dealers to provide a record of all gun sales. So if you buy a gun the authorities will know about it in some fashion. Open carry is allowed and the state does recognize a form of Stand Your Ground. So, smoke a joint and defend yourself!

West Virginia:

The State of West Virginia wants you to be able to carry a gun as you please. Its laws are very "Vermont-like." The unique difference being that some local governments do have gun restrictions in place.

Wisconsin:

In the State of Wisconsin there is a two day waiting period to purchase a gun, however open carry is generally permitted. Like other states silencers and such is prohibited and you can defend yourself in your home. Permits are handed out on a "shall issue" basis.

Wyoming:

Gotta love the State of Wyoming. Besides some of America's most beautiful country, the Second Amendment is sacrosanct.

Citizens and visitors are welcome to walk around strapped and be content. Carry a gun in Wyoming? Yes please! So the lesson here is in most states your right to bear arms is protected quite well. It is worth noting that the majority of America's urban areas restrict this right severely. It is also worth noting that the majority of America's urban areas are where most minorities live as well thus, leaving most minorities with an abridged version of the right to bear arms. Coincidence? Maybe, maybe not. The Second Amendment to the United States Constitution was ratified by the States as part of the Bill of Rights. Today, the Second Amendment's main advocate is the National Rifle Association. The NRA was originally organized to help teach shooting skills in light of statistics that showed American Civil War Union soldiers couldn't shoot worth a shit. It eventually morphed into what it is today. A powerful political lobby machine for gun rights. Along the way it has evolved itself into a great influencer on the election process as well.

As a result, because of the National Rifle Association no other Amendment to the United States Constitution has such an intense propaganda mechanism.

The Third Amendment to the United States Constitution

The text reads as such:

No Soldier shall, in time of peace be quartered in any house, without the consent of the Owner, nor in time of war, but in a manner to be prescribed by law.

This Amendment simply and plainly says that you have the right as a citizen not to have some United States Marine show up at your door and demand to raid your refrigerator right after you have come from the grocery store. James Madison, the United States Congress and the ratifying States left some wiggle room in times of war by adding the term "as prescribed by law." Meaning, if a war breaks out all bets are off. In many ways the Third Amendment to the United States Constitution is a follow up to the Second Amendment. Kind of a "kicker," of sorts. In that if you're holding a firearm anybody will have a moment of pause. The law's history goes back to Colonial times. Events like the Boston Tea Party and other uprisings of the day. The British tried to bully the American Colonies in many ways leading up the Declaration of Independence and the American Revolutionary War. By passing the so called "Intolerable Acts" the British fucked up real bad. In part the Intolerable Acts demanded Colonists room and board British troops. The Colonists were like, "What? Get the fuck outta here." This so pissed of everyone so much that in the United States Declaration of Independence, one of the many gripes to King George III was specifically in reference to the quartering of troops. So come Bill of Rights time the discussion shifted to forced government subjugation and troop quartering's role in it. Everyone in the United States Congress agreed the subject needed to be addressed in amendment form.

Among the state delegations in attendance for the drafting of the United States Constitution, the Commonwealth of Virginia had one of the loudest voices when it came to quartering troops. It was seen as a direct form of oppression. The rest of the push for the Third Amendment came from the Anti Federalists and ardent state's rights advocates. The Third Amendment to the United States Constitution was passed along with rest of the Bill of Rights in 1792.

The Fourth Amendment to the United States Constitution

The text reads as such:

The right of the people to be secure in their persons, houses, papers, and effects,[a] against unreasonable searches and seizures, shall not be violated, and no Warrants shall issue, but upon probable cause, supported by Oath or affirmation, and particularly describing the place to be searched, and the persons or things to be seized.

The Fourth Amendment says that a government official can't just take your shit at will. They better suspect you of something, tell a real good fucking story to a judge and be specific about their allegations. And get all of that shit in writing. Are there abuses in the system? Shit yeah, all the time. But even in those cases your rights are your rights.

Yes, Law and Order and these crime dramas make the shit look easy, but that is hardly the case in real life. Since Blacks were not citizens in the 1700s this is the White man's version of the Fourteenth Amendment to the United States Constitution. But we'll discuss that later. By default the Fourth Amendment had a dark side that lasted well into the Nineteenth

Century. For anybody who wasn't White you could not be "secure" in your own shit. Among others this included free Blacks. If you was a slave forget it. A slave's designation as property was compounded by exclusion as per the new law of the land. It was glass citizenship at best. The Fourth Amendment was a great legal tool to the argument of Manifest Destiny. A concept adopted early on in America's history that the borders of the United States stretched from "sea to shining sea." And who better than those citizens "secure" in their own shit to go out and tell those who are "not secure" in their own shit how it's gonna be. The non-secure would include, Blacks, Native Americans, Chinese and Mexicans among others. In the United States Congress since everybody in the room knew advanced citizenship would be popular and prized the Fourth Amendment was the gas that made the car run.

The Fourth Amendment to the Constitution is "value" citizenship. It was so valued that it was not going to be given out cavalierly. One could argue that the passage of the Fourth Amendment as part of the Bill of Rights was the fetus of the man that became the American Civil War. Which, in addition to many other things was a war where blood was spilled over non-White citizenship. Like the MasterCard commercial says, "American citizenship in the Nineteenth Century (if you were White?) Priceless!" The Fourth Amendment is the "Sistine Chapel" of the Bill of Rights. A true masterpiece. The Fourth Amendment is a common defense in many American courtrooms. If your rights were violated then the evidence is no good. This has created frustration for law enforcement at times but, tough shit. They get to live by the law just like everybody else. It should be noted that the United States Supreme has tightened definitions of terms like "search", "probable cause" and "reasonable." So, if you ever get jammed up make sure one of your attorney's first orders of business is doing a thorough examination of your Fourth Amendment protections. Or get another lawyer.

The Fifth Amendment to the United States Constitution

The text reads as such:

No person shall be held to answer for a capital, or otherwise infamous crime, unless on a presentment or indictment of a Grand Jury, except in cases arising in the land or naval forces, or in the Militia, when in actual service in time of War or public danger; nor shall any person be subject for the same offence to be twice put in jeopardy of life or limb; nor shall be compelled in any criminal case to be a witness against himself, nor be deprived of life, liberty, or property, without due process of law; nor shall private property be taken for public use, without just compensation.

The Fifth Amendment to the United States Constitution provides protection against the legal system and those who would choose to abuse it. The amendment says that if you have to stand up before The Man a grand jury has to give the ok. The Fifth Amendment also says you can't be tried for the crime twice. The system gets one shot at you, if they fuck it up they are out of luck. What is commonly called "double jeopardy." The Fifth Amendment further says you ain't gotta rat your own self out. Meaning you don't have to incriminate yourself. It also contains a due process provision so the authorities can't just take your shit away from you. Lastly, the Fifth Amendment says that the government can't take your shit and not pay you fairly for it. Commonly known as "eminent domain." This is the concept where the government all of a sudden finds use for your property, takes it but pays for it. Eminent domain is the government's "offer you can't refuse." The Fifth Amendment says the authorities have to pay you for it. The Fifth and Sixth Amendments to the United States Constitution were directly involved in creating the legal concept of "Miranda Rights." You've seen it on television and in the movies at one time or another. Generally, it says:

"You have the right to remain silent; anything you say or do may be used against you in a court of law. You have the right to an attorney, if you cannot afford an attorney one will provided at no costs to you." In 1966 the United States Supreme Court ruled that "not" making you aware of these rights was a violation of your Fifth Amendment rights. The Court basically said if you get arrested, from the giddy up, the cops have to advise you to just shut the fuck up until your lawyer shows up. The Fifth Amendment to the United States Constitution was adopted along with the rest of the Bill of Rights in 1792. The United States Supreme Court case was Miranda v. Arizona. We all know where Arizona is, but, who was Miranda? His full name is Ernesto Arturo Miranda. He was a laborer buy trade, but most of the time he was general fuck up. Born in 1941, he was from Mesa, Arizona. He was arrested in 1963 and charged with kidnapping, rape and armed robbery of a seventeen year old girl. He confessed to everything but his lawyer argued that his Fifth Amendment rights had been violated because the police didn't tell him that he had the right to just shut the fuck up. Again, from the giddy up.

The State of Arizona and the United States Government (represented by one Thurgood Marshall) argued that law enforcement didn't have the resources to provide that information to every person arrested. The United States Supreme Court said, "Fuck that, find the time." And just like that the Miranda Rights was born. Oh, and what happened to Ernesto? He was retried and convicted after his ex wife spilled all the beans so he wouldn't get custody of their child. After he got out of jail he made money autographing Miranda warning cards. However, like any violent fuckup he died violently. Ernesto got into a bar fight in Phoenix, Arizona and another crazy motherfucker stabbed his ass. So he gave his life for every dumb motherfucker who likes to commit violent crimes, still have rights and knows he's guilty as hell. On the other hand Miranda rights provide a tamper proof seal on your Fifth Amendment right not to incriminate yourself.

The Sixth Amendment to the United States Constitution

The text reads as such:

In all criminal prosecutions, the accused shall enjoy the right to a speedy and public trial, by an impartial jury of the State and district wherein the crime shall have been committed, which district shall have been previously ascertained by law, and to be informed of the nature and cause of the accusation; to be confronted with the witnesses against him; to have compulsory process for obtaining witnesses in his favor, and to have the Assistance of Counsel for his defence.

The Sixth Amendment is the constitutional bed you lay in when you actually get to court. It can be warm like the feeling you get on a cold winter's night or full of bugs and eat your ass alive. Protecting your rights in court is entirely up to you (and your attorney). The Sixth Amendment says your trial has to be fast, be done in front of everybody and heard by an "impartial" jury. I put impartial in quotation because the text of the Amendment says nothing about that jury consisting of your "peers." Again, Hollywood gets this wrong but there is a distinct difference between an impartial jury and a jury of your peers. Constitutionally there is no such thing as a "jury of your peers." Anyway, they have to tell you what you did and anyone who saw you do it has to show and tell his or her story. You also get to have people say nice things about you as well. And on top of all of that you get to be represented by an attorney whether you can afford it or not. Beware, however, like anything else in life. You get what you don't pay for. So the Sixth Amendment is like being given a fresh fruit basket right out of the grocer's produce section. One of the greatest examples of wrapping oneself in the warmth of the Sixth Amendment was O.J. Simpson. He had a speedy trial, an impartial jury (though one hardly made up of his peers), a great venue and thoroughly exercised his right to counsel. A team of serial litigators each of whom was a courtroom howitzer. Oh, and yep, he was acquitted. That shit don't work for everybody, however. There are still plenty of motherfuckers who get the bed bug version too. This is in part to shitty lawyers, overzealous prosecutors and, at times, not so impartial jurors.

The Seventh Amendment to the United States Constitution

The text reads as such:

In Suits at common law, where the value in controversy shall exceed twenty dollars, the right of trial by jury shall be preserved, and no fact tried by a jury, shall be otherwise re-examined in any Court of the United States, than according to the rules of the common law.

The summary of the Amendment is that you can sue someone in Civil Court and have the right for a jury to hear your beef. This was another Anti-Federalist instigation that has its roots in the Plantation South. The Seventh Amendment is a "property protection" clause. The funny thing is the "twenty dollar" thing is now measured in Twentieth Century terms. Which means the number is now a lot more than twenty dollars. The Seventh Amendment was adopted along with the rest of the United States Bill of Rights.

The Eighth Amendment to the United States Constitution

The text reads as such:

Excessive bail shall not be required, nor excessive fines imposed, nor cruel and unusual punishments inflicted.

The Eighth Amendment is what protects your ass after you are found guilty. It's set up so you get ONLY what you deserve regarding punishment. The history of the Amendment goes directly back to, once again, Henry VIII and his dick. Or, seen another way Anne Boleyn's pussy. All depending on what side of aisle you're sitting on. You see, Good ole, King Henry VIII thought that Lady Boleyn's pussy was so good he was willing to break up England's relationship with the Vatican. This, a result of wanting to get rid of Catherine of Aragon because Anne wouldn't just give up the pussy as a mistress (her stubbornness would lead to her downfall). If she was just "another piece of ass on the side like all the others there would be no Eighth Amendment to the United States Constitution. As a result, at the end of the Seventeenth

Century England has gone through several gyrations of commitment/ non-commitment to Catholicism. From Edward to Mary to Elizabeth to James to both Charles the First and Second and James II. Overall many English were wary and in some cases outright paranoid of Catholics. A commoner who would take advantage of the religious back and forth was a gentleman named Titus Oates.

He was key to the adoption of the Eighth Amendment as he was THE guy to suffer cruel and unusual punishment in such a way that boundaries had to be set as to societal consequences for crime. It also set a unique perspective as to future courts would see perjury or lying under oath. An offense which most courts in the United States take particularly onerously. Oates, born in 1649 would be the lead instigator in the so called "Popish Plot." An event that would see many innocent men executed as a result of his lies. This was a, albeit, much more bloody precursor to the American McCarthy hearings of the 1950s. The difference between Titus Oates and Senator McCarthy was McCarthy avoided jail. For his punishment Oates was sentenced to life imprisonment and to be whipped by the people five days every year while being dragged through the streets of London. They wanted to kill him but there was no death penalty for perjury at the time and this was the best punishment the judge could come up with. I guarantee that both he and anyone else who witnessed this never told another lie. Remember this story the next time you want to tell a lie. So, in many ways the Eighth Amendment could be called the "Titus Oates Amendment."

The big elephant in the room as it applies to the Eighth Amendment and the issue of cruel and unusual punishment is the death penalty. Government sponsored homicide has been debated from the early

72

colonial days to the present. The debate comes in all shapes and sizes. Is it morally sanitary for a civilized society? If so, what crimes should it apply to? Children? Mentally handicapped? Rapists (yes please)? Traitors? The history of the death penalty and the Eighth Amendment is part of America's constitutional complexities. Like everything else about the origins of the United States, the death penalty was a British "thing." In Colonial American, the earliest government institutional sponsored execution was in the Jamestown colony in the early 1600s. And the government has been killing their own ever since (not that some of those motherfuckers ain't deserve it, mind you). Today, thirty eight states will kill you if you do something really fucked up. Like killing your family because your toast was to brown. But if you really want to commit suicide by state sponsored homicide? Be in Texas, Oklahoma or Virginia. They'll be happy to kill you for your crime and do it expeditiously as well.

At the other end of the spectrum, the states of Michigan, Alaska and Hawaii have never had a death penalty statute. And Wisconsin has only executed on individual in its history. From 1972 to 1976 there were no executions in the United States at all. In 1972 the United States Supreme Court listened to a case and the Eighth Amendment's cruel and usual punishment language was cited. But it was what they didn't say that left opened the door to its return in 1976. The Court decided that the "process" of conviction and sentencing was flawed and that's just going too fucking far. What they didn't say, however, was that the death penalty in itself was unconstitutional. So, at the end of the day the Court said yes, governments can kill people, you just gotta find a more equitable process. It ain't gonna be as easy as it use to be. So the Eighth Amendment is there to make sure you only get what you deserve.

The Eighth Amendment to the United States Constitution was adopted along with the rest of the Bill of Rights.

The Ninth Amendment to the United States Constitution

The text reads as such:

The enumeration in the Constitution, of certain rights, shall not be construed to deny or disparage others retained by the people.

What? Yep, that's the Ninth Amendment to the United States Constitution. It is the "now that we're drunk let's superglue our faces to the wall" amendment. The Ninth Amendment is the "catch all" amendment insisted upon by the Anti-Federalists. However, its contents are already addressed in the Fourth, Fifth and even Sixth Amendments to the United States Constitution. And it is again covered by the subsequent Fourteenth Amendment.

The Ninth Amendment is the Constitution saying to the Federal Government "look, just because it's not mentioned in the other eight amendments don't mean there isn't other shit you also can't do." For example, the Government can't tell you what school to send your kids to (although they can and do say you have to send your kid to some kind of school), what kind of dog to own or even if you want to own a dog or not. The Ninth Amendment don't give you any extra shit, it just reinforces the shit you already have as it pertains to your civil rights. So the Ninth Amendment protects all Americans from "general" government overreach. It also reminds/warns the Federal Government to use a little fucking common sense as to how it thinks its citizens should live. The key word in the Ninth Amendment's text is "enumeration." Mathematically enumeration is simply a list separated into specific sets. Like one, two three, four or ten, twenty, thirty forty, etc. In the study of Political Theory the definition takes on a broader sense that says that the list does not have to closed-ended. The Ninth Amendment helps to keep political theory just that, "theory" when it comes to interpretation of the United States Constitution.

And, whether, purposively or accidental the Ninth Amendment is a great buffer for those who argue strict constructionist view of the Constitution and its adjoining amendments. Per the Constitution, the Government does have certain "enumerated powers." I'm not gonna cover them here but you can look them up. The point here is that those enumerated powers are in place to mostly protect the macro-society. Today the Ninth Amendment gets its teeth in the proposed, but not yet passed Enumerated Powers Act. The Enumerated Powers Act would require the United States Congress to specifically cite what part of the United States Constitution says they can do the shit they are about to do. What you should be asking yourself is "if it didn't pass what makes it relevant?" Its relevance lies in the fact that although it is not law many of its provisions have been adopted by the United States House of Representatives House Rules. So this is a law that is, in effect, active by proxy. But in the people's favor. The one person most responsible for the legislation is former United States House of Representatives member John Shadegg., a member of Republican Party representing the State of Arizona. The Ninth Amendment to the United States Constitution was ratified along with the rest of the Bill of Rights in 1791.

The Tenth Amendment to the United States Constitution

The text reads as such:

The powers not delegated to the United States by the Constitution, nor prohibited by it to the States, are reserved to the States respectively, or to the people.

While the Ninth Amendment protects not only your rights as stated in the United States Constitution but also your "implied" rights, the Tenth Amendment to the United States Constitution is a reminder to the Federal Government that the "only" powers it has are the ones stated in the United States Constitution. By default the Tenth Amendment also protects States rights and is defacto suppose to keep "big brother" out of your backyard. Of course, in reality, that shit ain't nowhere near the truth. Matter of fact, often times the Federal and State governments appear to collude when infringing upon your rights. The Federal Government does this by offering the States money with conditions. Anyway, the Tenth Amendment is suppose to limit Federal access to power to just what is mentioned in the Constitution. Like its sister, the Ninth Amendment it really isn't necessary. The first eight amendments and the surely the fourteenth cover the same shit. Ah, but those pesky Anti-Federalists weren't letting their opponents get away with shit. They basically said, "We don't care if we're repeating the same shit over again, put it in!" Besides James Madison, who as mentioned earlier is known as the Father of the Bill of Rights, others played influential roles in how the language of the Amendments were to be structured. In the case of the Tenth Amendment there were two individuals, Elbridge Gerry and Thomas Tudor Tucker. The former a member of the United States House of Representatives from the Commonwealth of Massachusetts and the latter a member from the State of South Carolina. Tucker was a Southern boy from Charleston, South Carolina by way of the island of Bermuda. Both of these men were strong advocates for the Bill of Rights and particularly the Tenth Amendment. Both men were interesting characters.

Elbridge Gerry would not only be an important member of the First and Second United States Congresses. He would also serve as Governor of the Commonwealth of Massachusetts but he would also serve as Vice President of the United States during the Administration of President James Madison. He remains a part of American lexicon through the term "gerrymander" or "gerrymandering." The term means to reorganize voting districts. Often by the current party in power. As Governor, he signed legislation redrawing voting districts in the Commonwealth and the press reported that one district looked like a salamander, which was New England-ized to "gerrymander." Congressman Tucker left his mark on American history that still stands to this day as well. Born in 1754 he was from a wealthy family in Bermuda. He would eventually settle in Charleston, South Carolina. Outside of the serving in the United States House of Representatives representing the State of South Carolina He would also serve in the State's House of Representatives. Considered a Patriot, like Gerry, he opposed the United States Constitution because he felt it gave too much power to a central government.

In addition to influencing the language of the Tenth Amendment, his legacy will forever be linked in the Executive Branch of the United States Government. He would serve as Treasurer of the United States for the Administration's of four Presidents. He would serve in this capacity for Presidents Thomas Jefferson, James Madison, James Monroe and John Quincy Adams. He served in that position until he died. For those of you who don't know who, or what the Treasurer of the United States is, let me tell you that you are very familiar with this government office. Every United States Federal Note (dollar bill regardless of denomination) has two signatures. One is the Secretary of the Treasury and the other is the Treasurer of the United States. Since 1949 the position has been held by a woman. In the Twenty First Century, in terms of political patronage the office is typically reserved for a Hispanic woman. This should give you an idea of how Executive jobs are handed out from Presidency to another. So, for all of you Hispanic mothers out there, you can groom your daughter to become Treasurer of the United States. I'm only half joking about that shit. Overall these two men had a quiet, yet lava flowing impact on the Bill of Rights.

Anyway, that wraps up the United States Bill of Rights. Of the original twelve amendments proposed these were the ten that got in. Of the two that didn't make it, one would become the Twenty Seventh Amendment to the United States Constitution (which we will get to) and the other is, technically, still pending (the Congressional Apportionment Amendment). Make no doubt about it the first ten Amendments and the Fourteenth Amendment are the sweet spot of American citizenship. Before we continue with the Eleventh Amendment to the United States Constitution it is worth noting the Legislative Branch of the Federal Government in a little more detail. In addition to being the first Ten Amendments to the United States Constitution they were also the last Amendments to be passed by the First and Second United States Congresses. So who were these rascals? Let's have a look.

Chapter 6

❧

The First and Second United States Congresses

O bviously, like George Washington the First United States Congress set many standards that still exist to this day. This Congress truly made world history. Besides passing the United States Bill of Rights several other milestones were set as well. Serving during the first two years of President George Washington's first term the First United States Congress had biggest task of setting rules to conduct the nation's business. They started out slow however. During the first month they basically didn't do shit and just sat around doing the grip and grin with each other. After that they got to work however, and, in a way today's United States Congress couldn't even come close to accomplishing. Yes there are many more members today, but still. So, what else did these gentlemen see through to completion? They established the Departments of War, State, Treasury and the Office of the United States Attorney General. They also set up the First Bank of the United States and agreed on a federal district just off of the Potomac River.

Also the States of North Carolina and Rhode Island would ratify the United States Constitution and join the Union as the twelfth and thirteenth states. The leadership was crucial to the First United States Congress. The President of the Senate was Vice President of the United States John Adams. He would go on to be the second President of the United States and also the first President to live in the White House. The Senate Pro Tempore was John Langdon. Langdon was a United States Senator from the State of New Hampshire. He made his money, along with his brother in shipping. An ardent Patriot, he hated the British because they restricted shipping and thusly his ability to make money. In addition to serving in the First United States Congress, Senator Langdon also served in the Continental Congress and the Congress of the Confederation. As a side note, he would help a young slave woman named Oney Judge. Judge was a slave owned by George and Martha Washington. She would run away to the North and Langdon was one of the individuals that helped her stay hidden and free. John Langdon would also serve as Governor of New Hampshire as well. In the United States House of Representatives the first Speaker of the House was Frederick Muhlenberg.

Congressman Muhlenberg was a theologian from a town called Trappe. It is a small suburb just northwest of Philadelphia in the Commonwealth of Pennsylvania. His father is considered to be one of the founders of the Lutheran Church in America. So his motivation to go against the British was simply religious tolerance. He was the first signer of the Bill of Rights. Additionally, he served in the Commonwealth of Pennsylvania House of Representatives as its Speaker. The Second United States Congress served in the second half of President George Washington's first term in office. It was during the Second United States

Congress that the states would ratify the United States Bill of Rights. Additionally they would pass legislation establishing the United States Post Office and the United States Mint. They would also set up America's first National Guard system and pass the first iteration of the Fugitive Slave Act in 1793. The Second United States Congress would welcome the Republic of Vermont and the Commonwealth of Kentucky (with the Commonwealth of Virginia's blessing) to the Union as well. The leadership consisted of Vice President John Adams as President of the Senate and Senator Richard Henry Lee as President Pro Tempore.

The Speaker of the House was Congressman Jonathan Trumbull Jr. Senator Lee was raised in an affluent family from the Commonwealth of Virginia. In addition to the United States Senate Lee also served in the Virginia legislature. He was also a signatory to the both the Declaration of Independence and the Articles of Confederation. Richard Henry Lee is most remembered as the man who put forth the resolution declaring the Colonies free from the British rule. So, basically it was Lee who came up with the idea to tell the English to go fuck themselves. In some ways, he could be considered America's "Father." As Speaker of the House Jonathan Trumbull was long in experience as a public servant. His father Jonathan Trumbull Sr. was Governor of Connecticut, both when it was a Colony and again as when it became a state. In addition Trumbull Jr. also serves as a trusted adviser to then General George Washington during the American Revolution War. After the war he would become an original member of the Society of the Cincinnati. He would also serve in the United States Senate as well as both Lieutenant Governor and Governor of Connecticut.

Chapter 7

❦

The Eleventh and Twelfth Amendments to the United States Constitution

The post Bill of Rights era gets off to the same kind of start that ended the Bill of Rights. Two amendments put in place as an overabundance of caution. This is, at least, one view of the Eleventh and Twelfth Amendments. In the case of the Eleventh Amendment its history goes directly back to the American Revolutionary War. It was also the first Amendment where the States told the Federal Government to go fuck itself. And further, it's also the first Amendment to directly challenge the original Constitution of the United States. In this case, specifically Article Three. The Eleventh Amendment also proved that ultimately, as political entities, the Legislative Branch of the United States Government can collude with individual state legislatures and effectively shut out the Executive Branch (meaning the President of the United States) and the United States Supreme Court. The Eleventh Amendment proved that America's real power lied in this corridor.

The United States Constitution has the State of Georgia directly to thank for the Eleventh Amendment. During the American Revolutionary War (1777) the State of Georgia purchased weapons from a gentleman gunrunner who lived in Charleston, South Carolina. His name was Robert Fuquhar. Mr. Fuquhar agreed to provide the goods and agree to an IOU from the State of Georgia. It didn't take long before Georgia politely said to Mr. Fuquhar, "fuck you, we're not paying you shit!" The State of Georgia had at two reasons for not wanting to pay Mr. Fuquhar his due cash receivables. First like many other states, they were deeply in debt and barely holding onto solvency. And second, there was resentment that Mr. Fuquhar was a "friend" of the British. You put that together and Georgia tells him to "fuck off!" Well the Eleventh Amendment would have its origins in the United States Supreme Court case Chisholm v Georgia. Fuquhar would die having never received his money, estimated at one hundred thousand pounds. It was surely enough money to argue about, that's a fact! The Chisholm part of the case is attributed to Alexander Chisholm. Mr. Chisholm was executor of Mr. Fuquhar's estate and sued on his behalf. That's only half the story because there only half a story to tell.

The State of Georgia never showed up to court. Citing "states rights" Georgia told the Federal Government that they have no jurisdiction over their affairs and that's that. "If as a state we want to fuck individuals out their shit, that our fucking business!" Note that there are still states that do this shit to this day. Does your? When Georgia didn't show up they had to give the win to Chisholm. The Supreme Court's ruling didn't still didn't mean shit to the State of Georgia. But, boy oh boy did it scare the shit out of the other states. Like Georgia all of the other states were in debt higher than giraffe pussy and if they were forced to pay back the people that they had PLANNED to fuck over, well, that shouldn't be the concern of a central government. The Eleventh Amendment is the other states backing Georgia's play and telling the Federal Government to mind your fucking business. The other thing the Supreme Court said was that Article Three of the Constitution gives the Government "ultimate" jurisdiction of everything. The Eleventh Amendment is the states saying back, "yeah right!" It's ironic that one of the Justices ruling in the case was the principal author of Article Three. Justice James Wilson. He would end up disagreeing with the very shit he originated.

That's like James Naismith not agreeing to the original rules he wrote when he invented basketball. Eventually, the State of Georgia was proved right. Messrs. Fuquhar, Chisholm, et al faded away having not been paid a nickel and the feeding frenzy that is the States fucking individuals over has been going strong ever since. So, go back and read the original text if you need to but that the real story behind this Amendment.

The timeline is as such:

1777- Georgia fucks over Fuquhar

1793-After sixteen years of getting fucked over, the issue of Fuquhar's money ends up in the Supreme Court. They say, "Pay the man." Georgia says, "Fuck you!"

1794-Knowing who they have fucked over and were about to fuck over the States got Congress to overwhelmingly agree that fucking individuals over is natural state right.

1795-The Eleventh Amendment was ratified by the required number of states when North Carolina put them over the top.

It's interesting to note that of all the states that made up the Union the State of New Jersey and the Commonwealth of Pennsylvania didn't give a fuck either way. Tennessee had just gained statehood and were to new to the game to have any kind of say. They were relegated to neo-state status and politically ignored at the time. So if you think you have a beef with yours or any other state and you want to sue them it will be an uphill battle. Unless that state "lets" you sue them the Federal Government won't and don't give a fuck. The Eleventh Amendment is the law that says that's just the way it is. All of this is further complicated by the fact the Eleventh Amendment steps all over your First Amendment right to petition the government for a redress of grievances. Crazy shit.

The Twelfth Amendment to the United States Constitution:

The text reads as such:

The Electors shall meet in their respective states, and vote by ballot for President and Vice-President, one of whom, at least, shall not be an inhabitant of the same state with themselves; they shall name in their ballots the person voted for as President, and in distinct ballots the person voted for as Vice-President, and they shall make distinct lists of all persons voted for as President, and all persons voted for as Vice-President and of the number of votes for each, which lists they shall sign and certify, and transmit sealed to the seat of the government of the United States, directed to the President of the Senate.

The President of the Senate shall, in the presence of the Senate and House of Representatives, open all the certificates and the votes shall then be counted.

The person having the greatest Number of votes for President, shall be the President, if such number be a majority of the whole number of Electors appointed; and if no person have such majority, then from the persons having the highest numbers not exceeding three on the list of those voted for as President, the House of Representatives shall choose immediately, by ballot, the President. But in choosing the President, the votes shall be taken by states, the representation from each state having one vote; a quorum for this purpose shall consist of a member or members from two-thirds of the states, and a majority of all the states shall be necessary to a choice. *And if the House of Representatives shall not choose a President whenever the right of choice shall devolve upon them, before the fourth day of March next following, then the Vice-President shall act as President, as in the case of the death or other constitutional disability of the President.*

The person having the greatest number of votes as Vice-President, shall be the Vice-President, if such number be a majority of the whole number of Electors appointed, and if no person have a majority, then from the two highest numbers on the list, the Senate shall choose the Vice-President; a quorum for the purpose shall consist of two-thirds of the whole number of Senators, and a majority of the whole number shall be necessary to a choice. But no person constitutionally ineligible to the office of President shall be eligible to that of Vice-President of the United States

The Twelfth Amendment cleaned up a lot of clutter not addressed in the original United States Constitution regarding Presidential (and

Vice Presidential) elections. The impetus for the Amendment was set in motion with the 1796 United States Presidential Election. John Adams ran against Thomas Jefferson. Mr. Jefferson finished second. It is the only United States Presidential Election that ended with a President and Vice President from opposing sides. Problem was in those days whoever finished second in the Presidential election automatically became Vice President. Exacerbating this was the fact that by now John Adams and Thomas Jefferson couldn't stand the site of each other. How would you like it if you had to work every day with the guy who kicked your ass?

In sports parlance this was analogous of hiring the Coach before you hire the General Manager. It didn't take the United States Congress long to figure out that shit just wouldn't get done if the two top motherfuckers can't get along. Imagine if the results of the 2012 Presidential Election ended with Barack Obama as President and Mitt Romney as Vice President. Wait? In hindsight that might not have been a bad thing. President Obama would have been resigned to "ain't this a bitch? I don't even like this motherfucker and I have to work with him for the next four years? I kicked HIS ass!" This was the checks and balances of it all. So, anyway, that visual is why the Amendment was adopted. By the way, as for what happened with the Presidency of John Adams? You guessed it. Vice President Jefferson got in his ass every chance he got. It's ironic that they died on the same date, July 4th. The Twelfth Amendment got through Congress very quickly in 1803. By June, 1804 it was ratified by a majority of the states. The Twelfth Amendment also changed the dynamics of the Electoral College. What is the Electoral College? The creation of the Electoral College "Africanized" the Presidential election process in the United States.

Hear me out on this. Every four years, as an American, when you cast your vote for President and Vice President of the United States you actually vote for an "Elector" who will cast your vote along with many others in a "pool." These Electors will then select a candidate for the entire pool. It is exactly the same as when a tribal leader in Africa makes a decision for the whole clan. It's ironic that this system works in a democratic process but the Africans have had such a difficult time adopting a democratic process! Life can be a trip sometimes. Nationwide the TOTAL Elector College membership is five hundred thirty eight delegates. That's it! This is the representation for three hundred and ten million. It's the "illusion of inclusion." They tried to get rid of it, once. After the 1968 Presidential Election. Republican Presidential Candidate Richard Nixon had way more electoral votes than his popular vote margin of victory warranted. He won forty three percent of the popular vote but garnered FIFTY SIX percent of the Electoral College vote. His opponent was Hubert Humphrey. This prompted the United States Congress to introduce a Constitutional Amendment abolishing the Electoral College and letting the people decide. One person, one vote. Period.

The Amendment passed in the United States House of Representatives with bipartisan support. In the United States Senate it failed to pass despite several votes and eventually died on the legislative vine, if you will. It was probably just as well. Opinion polls at the time showed support for state ratification was iffy at best. In more recent times your vote has been devalued by what is known as the National Popular Vote Interstate Compact. This is a U.S. State member organization that has agreed to vote for that individual who receives the most votes. Simple as that. Ah, but the distinction is that states' electors will vote for whoever wins the "national" vote, not necessary that particular states' vote. So, you could win Ohio and not win nationally so you lose Ohio too. The problem, in today's election world, is that the states that makeup the Compact (there are ten of them and Washington, D.C.) control sixty one percent of the total number of votes needed to get elected or one hundred sixty five of the two hundred seventy needed to get elected President. This shit is ripe for corruption. The system hasn't changed because both sides realize they each have an equal chance at crookedness. The two party system is the only game in town.

A third party candidate has virtually no chance of participating meaningfully in offering choice to voters. Even if they have better ideas. So if you're running for President of the United States your early goal is to lock up these ten states and Washington, D.C. then find the other measly thirty nine percent amongst the other forty states. This is the real game behind your vote. Yes, it's a lot easier said than done and those ten states ain't cheap either. Twenty First Century Presidential elections, financially speaking, are close to a billion (that's right, with a "b") dollars and rising.

The ten states that currently make up the Compact:

Maryland
New Jersey
Illinois
Hawaii
Washington
Commonwealth of Massachusetts
District of Columbia

Vermont

California

Rhode Island

New York

And this is where a majority of Presidential campaign funds are spent. It is no coincidence that the above list makes up some of the wealthiest States in America. Shit, the State of California is among the top ten economies in the world! At the end of the day the Electoral College and its concept is Democracy's version of kidney stones. You can live with them, but "damn!"

Chapter 8

❧

The Reconstruction Amendments, The Thirteenth, Fourteenth and Fifteenth Amendment to the United States Constitution

The Thirteenth, Fourteenth and Fifteenth Amendments to the United States Constitution are three of the most important Amendments on the books. They can also be called the "Malcolm X Amendments because of the impact they had on Black folks in America. Specifically, the Thirteenth Amendment abolished slavery in the United States. The Fourteenth Amendment (among other things) granted full citizenship regardless of race and the Fifteenth granted the right to vote regardless of race (but interestingly not gender). All three were passed with generous help of the so called Radical Republicans. But more about them later. It is questionable whether the Fourteenth or the Fifteenth Amendment would have appeared in its current form had President Abraham Lincoln not been assassinated. Mr. Lincoln was prepared to appease many Whites in the South after the war and would have gone to great lengths to stunt citizenship for Blacks immediately.

For him, emancipation and slavery was a big step and the newly reunited nation had to digest that reality before moving on to other goals. His second term Vice President Andrew Johnson felt the same way when he ascended to the Presidency. Radical Republicans would not be denied however and Andrew Johnson threats to slow progress led to his impeachment. Of the three the Fourteenth would have the most profound and lasting legacy on American jurisprudence. Landmark United States Supreme Court cases Plessey v Ferguson (1896) and Brown v Board of Education (1954) both lean heavily on the Fourteenth Amendment for justification. We will get a chance to examine the people, events and circumstances that made them all come about. So what was the Reconstruction Era? It was that period in the Nineteenth Century that stretched from the end of the American Civil War until after the President Election of 1876. America dealt with the end of the War, the plight of freed, yet still disenfranchised Blacks and reintegration of the Southern States back into the Union. The Era would stretch from the Presidency's of Abraham Lincoln to Rutherford B. Hayes. In terms of power the Legislative Branch of the United States Government would dominate over the other branches.

Mostly through the prism of the amendment process. More to the point, for those of you who don't thing midterm national elections don't matter the Reconstruction is your case study. The Midterm Elections of 1866 changed the direction of the United States and set in motion a whole new sociological norm. And while it is considered a historical failure the Era's legacy is the closest thing to treating "civil" rights as "human" rights in the entire United States Constitution. The reality of Reconstruction on the ground however was a wholly different reality. The North relied heavily on the military to keep the defeated in line. And most Northerners wanted to South's inclusion back into the Union to be painful. Northerners sent emissaries south to represent their interests (derisively referred as "carpetbaggers" by Southerners). These folks got help from less loyal, moral and ethically challenged Southerners (called "scalawags" by yet other Southerners) who saw a chance for power and profit. The funny thing about these Radical Republicans was as bad as they bothered the shit out of Andrew Johnson they would have done the same thing to Abraham Lincoln.

As early as 1862 President Lincoln had wanted to re-colonize freed slaves to Central and/or South America. He met with Black leaders of the day and basically told them, "look, if you just away we'll help you re-locate, take over another country and support along the way. Lincoln always felt that Blacks would never get a fair shake in America, even post emancipation. Blacks, were like, "Oh no! Another trip? Fuck that shit!" So, Black life post Civil War under President would have been very different given his real attitudes. Which was Union first (rightfully so, mind so) and Blacks as we get to them. President also wanted to compensation Southern slave owners for their lost of slaves as a result of emancipation. Reconstruction would finally fall with the Presidential Election of 1876 the winner Rutherford B. Hayes.

The Thirteenth Amendment to the United States Constitution

The text reads as such:

Section 1. Neither slavery nor involuntary servitude, except as a punishment for crime whereof the party shall have been duly convicted, shall exist within the United States, or any place subject to their jurisdiction.

Section 2. Congress shall have power to enforce this article by appropriate legislation.

The saga of the passage of the Thirteenth Amendment is told well in Doris Kearns Goodwin's Team of Rivals and to a lesser extent Steven Spielberg's Lincoln (but still good in its own right, don't get it twisted). Both works of art highlight well President Lincoln's determination to be done, once and for all, with the issue of slavery. So we know what the Amendment does on the surface. What else does it do? Today, the Amendment is cited in sex crime and sex trafficking cases. The Thirteenth Amendment also clears the way for the United States prison system to systematically sustain pseudo economies through the labor of convicted felons. This is the "fleas come with the dog" Amendment. Passage of the Thirteenth Amendment effectively muted the Three Fifths Compromise agreed to in the original Constitution. The Compromise defined Blacks as three fifths of a person as it related to population and representation in the United States House of Representatives. Like President Lincoln's Emancipation Proclamation the Thirteenth Amendment also failed to live up to printed hype. The realities of life for Blacks in America at the time hardly changed and where it did, in some cases, it was for the worst. Although the Thirteenth Amendment abolished slavery and indentured servitude they were left with the question of "What now?" President

Lincoln and later the President Andrew Johnson and the Radicals Republicans were left to ask, "What the fuck do we do with all of these motherfuckers now that they don't work for us for free anymore?" For post American Civil War White America the question regarding Blacks was about Black freedom, citizenship and voting rights while giving or acknowledging equality, social or intellectual.

This ideology began after the War and continues in many ways to this day. The Thirteenth Amendment ended slavery on the one hand and began the era of second class citizenship for Blacks in perpetuity. Former slaves became sharecroppers and many Southern states passed laws that restricted movement, living space and job opportunities for Blacks. This ensured a chokehold on real participatory citizenship. In the United States Congress some argued that freeing Blacks from slavery would (God forbid) lead to citizenship and along with that dreadfully the right to bear arms. The very thought of armed former slaves scared the shit of some of them. And these were Northern anti-slavery Whites! The man who brought an amendment to the floor of the United States House of Representatives was an abolitionist named James Mitchell Ashley. Congressman Ashley was born in the western part of the Commonwealth of Pennsylvania. He would go on to represent the State of Ohio in the United States House of Representatives. He would also serve as the Governor of the Montana Territory prior to statehood.

In the United States Congress, in addition to bringing what would become the Thirteenth Amendment to the floor he would also be the man who would initiate impeachment proceedings against President Andrew Johnson. Congress Ashley was with John Brown's widow the day of his execution. The ambiguity of citizen status left by the lack of language in the Thirteenth Amendment pushed the United States Congress to pass the first Civil Rights Act (1866). The legislation guaranteed citizenship and all its defined rights for all Blacks. It did not include the right to vote. In 1875 and 1965 there would be two other "Civil Rights Acts." America just couldn't seem to get it right. Further, Southerners argued that "the Federal Government can guarantee freedom, but you can't tell what the definition of freedom is. And we choose to say Whites and Blacks and two different levels of freedom." This point led directly to further clarification that became the Fourteenth and Fifteenth Amendments. Note that since neither the Thirteenth, Fourteenth or Fifteenth Amendments mentioned nothing about the status of women in American this would lead to the Nineteenth Amendment. But more on that later.

The Thirteenth Amendment to the United States Constitution was ratified by the States in December, 1865 after having been passed by the Thirty Eighth United States Congress. This was eight months after President Abraham Lincoln's assassination under the gun of John Wilkes Booth. It was over sixty years between passage of the Twelfth and Thirteenth Amendments. This is the longest length of time between passages of Amendments to this day. It's ironic that the State of Georgia (again) was responsible for putting the States over the top regarding ratification. Lastly, the number "thirteen" would leave it legacy on the United States Constitution as this was the third proposed amendment to, if passed, would have become the Thirteenth Amendment. The "first" Thirteenth Amendment would have been the Titles of Nobility Amendment and the "second" would have been the Corwin Amendment. Both are discussed in the section of Tropospheric Politics on Amendments that didn't make the cut.

The Fourteenth Amendment to the United States Constitution

The text reads as such:

Section 1. All persons born or naturalized in the United States, and subject to the jurisdiction thereof, are citizens of the United States and of the State wherein they reside. No State shall make or enforce any law which shall abridge the privileges or immunities of citizens of the United States; nor shall any State deprive any person of life, liberty, or property, without due process of law; nor deny to any person within its jurisdiction the equal protection of the laws.

Section 2. Representatives shall be apportioned among the several States according to their respective numbers, counting the whole number of persons in each State, excluding Indians not taxed. But when the right to vote at any election for the choice of electors for President and Vice President of the United States, Representatives in Congress, the Executive and Judicial officers of a State, or the members of the Legislature thereof, is denied to any of the male inhabitants of such State, being twenty-one years of age, and citizens of the United States, or in any way abridged, except for participation in rebellion, or other crime, the basis of representation therein shall be reduced in the proportion which the number of such male citizens shall bear to the whole number of male citizens twenty-one years of age in such State.

Section 3. No person shall be a Senator or Representative in Congress, or elector of President and Vice President, or hold any office, civil or military, under the United States, or under any State, who, having previously taken an oath, as a member of Congress, or as an officer of the United States, or as a member of any State legislature, or as an executive or judicial officer of any State, to support the Constitution of the United States, shall have engaged in insurrection or rebellion against the same, or given aid or comfort to the enemies thereof. But Congress may, by a vote of two-thirds of each House, remove such disability.

Section 4. The validity of the public debt of the United States, authorized by law, including debts incurred for payment of pensions and bounties for services in suppressing insurrection or rebellion, shall not be questioned. But neither the United States nor any State shall assume or pay any debt or obligation incurred in aid of insurrection or rebellion against the United States, or any claim for the loss or emancipation of any slave; but all such debts, obligations and claims shall be held illegal and void.

Section 5. The Congress shall have power to enforce, by appropriate legislation, the provisions of this article.

The Fourteenth Amendment to the United States Constitution is the granddaddy of Amendments. It encompasses elements of entire Bill of Rights and defines the foundation of American citizenship. It is the most cited of all Amendments in arguments before the United States Supreme Court.

The Fourteenth Amendment has been involved in such landmark cases as Plessey v Ferguson (1896) to Brown v Board of Education of Topeka (1954) to Roe v Wade (1973) and even Bush v Gore (2000). Like the First Amendment there are five sections to the Amendment. The

Fourteenth Amendment is the basis of the immigration argument and specifically defines what a citizen is in America. Among those definitions is anyone born in the United States regardless of the citizenship of that baby's parents is a citizen of the United States. Today, Republican and Democratic positions on the subject of illegal immigration lie solely on this Constitutional language. On to the specifics of the Amendment itself.

Section One of the Fourteenth Amendment is a conflagration of the Fourth, Fifth and Sixth Amendments, but with a kicker. It says everybody here is a fucking citizen of the United States and, as such, afforded all of the rights of a citizen. Further the Fourteenth Amendment makes it clear to the individual states that these rights cannot be fucked with. Which is ironic because Section One of the Fourteenth Amendment spits in the face of the Eleventh Amendment. Section One also gave teeth to the Civil Rights Act of 1866. Citizenship for Blacks was now unquestioned. The Citizenship Clause didn't mean shit to Native Americans however since their status as citizens was ambiguous at best. It would take the Indian Citizenship Act of 1924 to straighten that shit out. Helped in no small part by future Vice President of the United States and a Native American of the Kansas based Kaw tribe Charles Curtis in his capacity as United States Senator. Section Two of the Fourteenth Amendment re-clarifies and nullifies the Three Fifths Compromise in the original United States Constitution. Now that Blacks are citizens they will count as one vote just like everybody else. There were caveats attached, however. It applied ONLY to males over the age of twenty one years. It did not mention women or Native Americans. Matter of fact the Fourteenth Amendment was used by both sides to deny women the right to vote.

As mentioned in my first book Three Blind Mice, the United States Supreme Court case of Minor v Happersett (1875) was a landmark case that specifically said women do not have a right to vote AND that the right to vote was not necessarily a foundation of citizenship and liberty in these United States (except if you're a man). State of Missouri resident Virginia Minor sued the Registrar, Mr. Happersett for denying her the right to vote in the 1872 Presidential Election. Section Three of the Fourteenth Amendment says "look if you are talking and doing subversive shit behind our back you can't be a member of the United States Congress." Period. That's it. Sections Four and Five of the Fourteenth Amendment deal with Government's responsibility, its debt and the fact that the United States Congress can enforce what the fuck they just said respectively. Section Four also got the Federal Government off the hook for ever having to compensate former slaveholders for their slaves. It was a smooth fucking move. Although the Fourteenth Amendment guaranteed citizenship and civil rights to Blacks it did not address "voting rights."

This would be addressed in the Fifteenth Amendment. In 1868 Secretary of State William Seward would certify the Fourteenth Amendment as part of the United States Constitution. This was a very contentious state ratification process. As it was a few states would be very late to the "all men are created equal" party. The last place finisher would the Commonwealth of Kentucky. The legislature did not ratify the Fourteenth Amendment until 1976! Not a good showing for a state proud of their thoroughbreds. Even the State of Mississippi passed the Fourteenth in 1870. What does that say? It's also worth noting that it took the Reconstruction Acts to allow the Federal Government to take over many state governments militarily and put their own people in. But

America should be proud. It was a defining moment in the ideology of government/citizens relations. Especially the Due Process and Equal Protection Clauses in Section One. They are the "teeth" of the entire Fourteenth Amendment.

The Fifteenth Amendment to the United States Constitution

The text reads as such:

Section 1. The right of citizens of the United States to vote shall not be denied or abridged by the United States or by any State on account of race, color, or previous condition of servitude.

Section 2. The Congress shall have power to enforce this article by appropriate legislation.

The Fifteenth Amendment to the United States Constitution overwhelmingly gave Blacks the right to vote. Ultimately, it is the Michael Jordan of voting rights acts (pun intended). The history of the Amendment is unique to the others because it specifically addresses citizen "political rights." While its perceived need came as a result of the end of slavery in America, it also applied to ALL citizens. One of the questions we'll look at is WHO was defined as citizens. Also there is the judicial evolution of the Fifteenth Amendment post passage and ratification.

Along with the Thirteenth and Fourteenth Amendments, the Fifteenth Amendment would be the trifecta to give American Blacks the other "two-fifths" the evaded them in the Three-Fifths Compromise written into the original United States Constitution. So let's get on with it. Don't get it twisted that the Radical Republicans were not all about "all men are created equal" when it came to the Fifteenth Amendment. At this juncture in American history with the election of Ulysses S. Grant in 1868 the Republican Party controlled both houses of the United States Congress and the Executive Branch. Since the Fourteenth Amendment said nothing about voting rights Republicans knew that the best way to secure long term votes from Blacks was to enfranchise them in the power sharing mechanism. For the United States Congress the plan was simple. Give Blacks the vote and then get President Grant to enforce their actions which he was more than happy to do. The plan worked too, until President Hoover fucked over Blacks by reneging on campaign promises made during the 1928 election. Subsequent President Franklin D. Roosevelt's New Deal would entice Blacks to vote Democrat until this day. Anyway.

Some Radical Republicans did not think the language in the Fifteenth went far enough and they would be proven right as well with the passage of the Voting Rights of 1965. Other casualties in the fight to pass the Fifteenth Amendment included the American Women's Suffrage Movement. While the woman suffrage movement had been aligned with abolition and ending of slavery some in the movement felt that if Blacks can specifically have the right to vote then why can't women right beside them and right now. This led to a split of the movement into two ideology factions. Led by Elizabeth Cady Stanton and Susan B. Anthony, one faction wanted action on gender neutral voting protections immediately. The other faction wanted a more cautious approach and supported a "one step at a time" version. They were led by the ironically fiery Lucy Stone and Henry Browne Blackwell. Eventually they would each have their day with the passage of the Nineteenth Amendment to the United

States Constitution. The Fifteenth Amendment also has some unexpected repercussions. It would lead to the end of Reconstruction and usher in the era of "political marginalization" for American Blacks that would last until the 1960s. Remember this was the 1870s.

After the Amendment's passing Blacks, both free and former slaves didn't hesitate to exercise their now constitutional right to vote. The Jackie Robinson of Black voters was a gentleman named Thomas Mundy Peterson. Mr. Peterson was the first Black person in the history of the United States to vote in an election after passage of the Fifteenth Amendment to the United States Constitution. Hailing from the State of New Jersey (born in Metuchen, raised in Perth Amboy), today March 31st is now a state holiday known as Thomas Mundy Peterson Day. This also makes him the first Black man to have annual holiday named after him. Much respect to Dr. Martin Luther King Jr., however. The Fifteenth Amendment would also lead directly to violence. In the South passage of the Amendment galvanized Whites like never before. Groups like the Ku Klux Klan (KKK) would evolve quickly. Southern Whites knew two things during Reconstruction; one, they knew Union troops couldn't stay there forever and two, as long as they denied Blacks the right to vote, disenfranchisement would follow. The most notable instance would be the Colfax Massacre, which occurred Easter Sunday, 1873. Named after the seat of Grant Parish in the State of Louisiana, the incident resulted in hundreds of dead.

Mostly Black and most killed after they had surrendered. With the 1872 Louisiana Gubernatorial Election as a backdrop, all types were involved. Participants included Democrats, Republicans, Carpetbaggers, Scalawags and others of ill repute. Just as the Radical Republicans has predicted, Blacks rewarded their passage of the Reconstruction Acts with unwavering loyalty. During the statewide elections in the State of Louisiana in 1872 Republicans were staunchly supported by the Black citizenry. White citizens supported the Democrats and in this election each voted for their governor. So what? Except the Democrats showed up at the courthouse with rifles and at least one small cannon. After the murders many were arrested by justice would be served. In what was to be the first of many instances, the Southern white perpetrators were eventually acquitted of the killings of all these Black people. The case would even make its way to the United States Supreme Court as United States v Cruikshank, 1876. The Court would issue rulings that further defined the First, Second and Fourteenth Amendments. The right of Blacks to vote and what lengths White Southerners would go to prevent that vote would be an unfortunate part of the Fifteenth Amendment's legacy.

Chapter 9

❧

Post Reconstruction Amendments, Sixteen Through Twenty

The Sixteenth Amendment to the United States Constitution:

The text reads as such:

The Congress shall have power to lay and collect taxes on incomes, from whatever source derived, without apportionment among the several States, and without regard to any census or enumeration.

The Sixteenth Amendment is the famed "Income Tax" Amendment. This is the Amendment that guarantees that the United States Government gets to share in your happiness every time you get paid. The best part about it is that they don't even trust you to give it to them.

Every payday they just jack your fucking check for their share. They are happy to give you a refund if they took too much but we all pay upfront. This is the Amendment that made accountants famous. And when you combine the Internal Revenue Service and the Federal Reserve Bank (created by the Federal Reserve Act of 1913) you had the recipe for the number one financed organization in the entire world in no time. From then on these two entities would be directly responsible for every stock market crash in America to this day. The Sixteenth would also dramatically change the role of the Internal Revenue Service. Their workload would triple with the passage of the Revenue Act of 1913, passed on the back of the Sixteenth Amendment. What all of this legislation meant was that in 1914 if a couple made four thousand dollars they paid one percent. Single individuals had a three thousand dollar threshold. The surprising figure is that these citizens represented only one percent of the population in the United States at the time. By 1915 the United States was making more money than they had ever seen. The Sixteenth Amendment would directly affect world history through financing America's "reach."

Two of the men important to the legislative events of the early 1900s? United States Senator Nelson Aldrich and United States Congressman Oscar Underwood. Mr. Aldrich was Senior Senator from the State of Rhode Island. His grandson was Nelson Rockefeller, Vice President of the United States under the Ford Administration. He would not only be important to passage of the Sixteenth Amendment to the United States Constitution but also in establishing the Federal Reserve System. He made his money the old fashion way, slave labor. Except in this case it was in the Belgian Congo where King Leopold II had effective slave in place to extract the country's abundant natural resources, specifically mining and rubber production. Oscar Underwood served in both the United States House of Representatives and the United States Senate. Born in the Commonwealth of Kentucky, He served politically the State of Alabama in Washington, D.C. Despite being a Democrat from the South in the early Twentieth Century he strongly opposed groups like the Ku Klux Klan (what a stupid fucking name). He ran for President of the United States in 1924. The glue that makes the Sixteenth Amendment hold itself together?

The United States House of Representatives' House Ways and Means Committee. One can think of them as the "Commission" of the United State Congress. All tax writing initiatives begin with this committee. Since the United States House of Representatives is responsible for the government's finances, this committee alone decides how the United States Government funds itself. They are the "Gangstas of the World!" This fact is without dispute. As a result its members are quite influential and powerful and play a major role in the history of the United States. The aforementioned Oscar Underwood was also, at one time, the Chairman of Ways and Means. The Sixteenth Amendment to the United States Constitution became Utah and the Commonwealth of Virginia rejected it outright. Utah was a unique case because they had only been granted statehood a little over a decade earlier. The Mormons had been trying to become part of the United States since the 1850s and many felt that they didn't want to pay more money through taxation after getting fucked over for so long. Although one could argue that they brought that on themselves with that polygamy bullshit. Either way, they decided to play political ball and not make a fuss.

The Seventeenth Amendment to the United States Constitution

The text reads as such:

The Senate of the United States shall be composed of two Senators from each State, elected by the people thereof, for six years; and each

Senator shall have one vote. The electors in each State shall have the qualifications requisite for electors of the most numerous branch of the State legislatures.

When vacancies happen in the representation of any State in the Senate, the executive authority of such State shall issue writs of election to fill such vacancies:

Provided, That the legislature of any State may empower the executive thereof to make temporary appointments until the people fill the vacancies by election as the legislature may direct.

This amendment shall not be so construed as to affect the election or term of any Senator chosen before it becomes valid as part of the Constitution.

The Seventeenth Amendment to the United States Constitution allowed YOU to elect your United States Senator through the popular vote as opposed to them being appointed from a given states legislature. This was an amendment directly concerned about your "citizenship" rights much like the Fifteenth Amendment to the United States Constitution. The amusing part of the Seventeenth Amendment's journey was it actually passing in the United States Senate. The individual Senators in Washington, D.C. at the time of debate on the Amendment had a cushy setup and didn't want the system to be fucked with. But they would not win the day.

It's also interesting to note that the original United States Constitution mandated that Senators be directly elected/selected by a State legislature, not the people. The Founding Fathers figured that picking Senators by legislative body kept intact the idea of states' rights. Especially in counterbalance to the makeup of the United States House of Representatives which was and is directly elected by the people. Shit, the whole reason for a Senate at all was to keep tabs on those bastards in the House in the first place. Much of the idea of a Senate was based on the British House of Lords, but without the lineage bullshit. In drafting the original United States Constitution legislative election of Senators was the brainchild of the Anti-Federalists. Their fear of a powerful central government led them reason that Senators chosen by the legislature would be in Washington, D.C. to represent the "State," not necessarily the people. What's the difference? Senators would be working for the State power structure, not the citizens themselves. Over time, however, problems would arise that would lead to the passage of the Seventeenth Amendment. At times State legislatures couldn't agree on who should represent them. Some individuals were accused of "buying" Senate seats.

When drafting the original Constitution one individual did argue for popular elections. His name was James Wilson. James Wilson was a Founding Father and signer of the Declaration of Independence. President George Washington would nominate him as one of the original Justices' to the United States Supreme Court. Wilson also proposed the "Three-Fifth Compromise." Another individual that stood out in the debate over the Seventeenth Amendment was Elihu Root. He was so pissed off at the passage of the Amendment that he decided not to run for reelection post passage. He would also serve as Secretary of War and Secretary of State in the course of his long public service. The Seventeenth Amendment also allowed for Governors to fill vacancies until elections could be held. The lure of corruption is also a big point made by critics of the Amendment. This provision alone has led to many calling for a repeal of the Amendment. It's ironic that the Seventeenth Amendment in effect repealed portions of the original United States Constitution and some have called the Amendment unconstitutional from the giddy up. The Seventeenth Amendment to the United States Constitution was passed in the United States House of Representatives in 1911.

In a reminder about how racist America was in the early Twentieth Century, the House version included a rider that barred the Federal Government from acting on racial discrimination cases when they occurred. This was to protect those States intent on marginalizing select citizens' rights. The Senate version passed in 1912 did not include the rider. The Amendment passed in 1913 after the House decided to drop the rider. Both houses realized that the Amendment was vague enough that the States still had plenty of room to fuck over whoever they wanted. This would partly be rectified by the Twenty Fourth Amendment to the United States Constitution which will be discussed later. Which brings us to the Eighteenth Amendment to the United States Constitution.

The Eighteenth Amendment to the United States Constitution

The text reads as such:

Section 1. After one year from the ratification of this article the manufacture, sale, or transportation of intoxicating liquors within, the importation thereof into, or the exportation thereof from the United States and all the territory subject to the jurisdiction thereof for beverage purposes is hereby prohibited.

Section 2. The Congress and the several States shall have concurrent power to enforce this article by appropriate legislation.

Section 3. This article shall be inoperative unless it shall have been ratified as an amendment to the Constitution by the legislatures of the several States, as provided in the Constitution, within seven years from the date of the submission here to the States by the Congress.

The Eighteenth Amendment introduced Prohibition to the United States as Federal law. It outlawed alcohol. You couldn't make it, sell it or ship it.

Ironically the law didn't say you couldn't drink it or have it for private consumption, however. Lawmakers figured if you couldn't legally get it you wouldn't get it. What they didn't count on was America's appetite for the libation by any means necessary. The Eighteenth Amendment did more for organized crime in the United States than any single event since slavery. One could argue that its repeal via the Twenty First Amendment to the United States Constitution was, in part, because organized crime was crowding the Federal Government when it came fucking people over. Yes, that is a generalization but not far from the truth. Names like Al Capone, Frank Nitti, Myer Lansky, Charles "Lucky" Luciano, Carlo Gambino, Salvatore Marazano and a host of others all became famous as a result by the inadvertent sanctioning of the Eighteenth Amendment. The Amendment introduced a whole new party in the form of speakeasies, social clubs and other private gatherings. The Amendment itself was pushed by the Temperance Movement of the early Twentieth Century. Basically a hodgepodge of elitist that thought everyone should live by their rules. These folks felt that alcohol was an abomination to society that led to crime, divorce, abuse and violence. Which was probably true.

They just didn't count on what would happen in reality. It was a mistake indeed. The Eighteenth Amendment would put the "roaring" in the Roaring Twenties as the decade of the 1920s was known. It can be argued that the Eighteenth Amendment even produced a President of the United States in the form of John F. Kennedy. His father, Joseph Kennedy made much of his money bootlegging during the Prohibition era. Even funnier was the fact that Washington, D.C. was awash in liquor while legislators were trying to take it away from everyone else. To give the Eighteenth Amendment its teeth, the United States Congress passed the National Prohibition Act commonly known as the Volstead Act. The act gave enforcement power to Amendment. But before we get to that though, back to the Temperance Movement. The idea of Temperance in America goes back to its founding. From an alcohol consumption point of view the idea was simple. Drinking is bad; therefore, society should not drink. The hope was that everyone could in some form of delusional utopia. As the Italians would say, "che a una stronzata!" That's bullshit. Even if it was achievable it would have only applied to rich, White men. The movement faded out with the outbreak of the American Civil War.

Slavery and preserving the Union were the tantamount issues of the day. The Temperance Movement roared back to life with the election of President Rutherford B. Hayes and the end of Reconstruction. In the early Twentieth Century the movement was politically strong enough to force the passage of the Eighteen Amendment. In Twenty First Century American politics the National Rifle Association uses the same play-book. One of the main influencers of the Temperance Movement was an organization known as the Anti Saloon League. It was founded as a state society in Oberlin, Ohio. In terms of lobbying clout these guys are originals. Hall of Famers for sure. The Anti Saloon League basically invented K Street, Washington, D.C. as it exists today. They didn't care if you drank or not they just cared how you voted. The NRA takes the same approach on gun rights. They were very strong in the South and among a wide variety of religious organizations. Its main figurehead and leader was Wayne Wheeler. And this guy was a trip. He started out as a field secretary in the Anti Saloon League not long after graduating from Oberlin College. He became President of the ASL and expertly exerted political pressure on every Congressperson, politely and otherwise.

His leadership of the ASL turned the organization into a first of its kind D.C. pressure pusher. It was effective because it focused on one issue only. A Federal mandate on the banning of alcohol. Wayne Wheeler had access to every nook and cranny of the Power D.C. From the President down to a Congressional Page. The ironic thing about Mr. Wheeler is that for a man that fought about the ills of alcohol on health and society he died at fifty seven! And it was from exhaustion of the fight. The Anti Saloon League experienced its own irony as well. With violent crime and corruption out of control as a result of the Eighteenth Amendment combined with the Stock Market Crash of 1929 they knew appeal of the Amendment was only a matter of time. Mr. Wheeler and the ASL would eventually concede and, ironically enough back Franklin D. Roosevelt and the Democrats in the Presidential Election of 1932. Yes, while Mr. Roosevelt was campaigning about ending the Great Depression and the New Deal he was quietly pushing on ending Prohibition as well. So the passage of the Twenty First Amendment and the fact that the ASL's Southern faction would never stop supporting the Ku Klux Klan greatly diminished their power.

The Anti Saloon League does exist in the Twenty First Century in the form of the American Council on Alcoholic Problems. And they're still pushing the same old tired bullshit to the American people. Just nobody's paying attention. So, National Rifle Association, be careful what you wish for. You might just get it. The National Prohibition Act, or commonly known as the Volstead Act was the devil in the details after fact of the Eighteenth Amendment. Eliot Ness was to gain fame as a result of the Volstead Act. The Volstead Act allowed law enforcement to say "if I catch you selling or drinking alcohol Imma put yo ass in jail!" What Congress and the Prohibitionists didn't expect was that on the streets cops quickly realized that the shit ain't worth dying over. Many policemen quickly realized that accepting payoffs was not only safer but made Christmas a whole better for the whole family. President Woodrow Wilson vetoed the act when it arrived on his desk. But, in a nod to the power of Wayne Wheeler and the Anti Saloon League it was overridden the by the United States House of Representatives the same day. The United States Senate followed suit the next day. President Wilson primarily objected because the bill also included a wartime prohibition of alcohol.

This was an early example of a powerful United States Congress trumping a powerful United States President. The Volstead Act gave the Federal Government wide powers to enforce the Eighteenth Amendment. And yes, this led to abuses of that power. But society has a way of determining for itself which laws make sense and which ones just don't work no matter how those in power try to make it work. Social acceptance of illegal drinking was so widespread that the Government finally had to relent with the passage of the Twenty First Amendment. In the Twenty First Century the same phenomena is occurring with marijuana. The Act itself was named after Andrew Volstead. Volstead was a member of the United States House of Representatives from the State of Minnesota. A Republican, he was head of the House Judiciary Committee and a primary lackey of Wayne Wheeler and the Anti Saloon League. It was Wheeler who drafted most of the text of the bill while

Volstead acted as his inside man promoting, sponsoring, supporting and shepherding the bill through the United States Congress. What is the legacy of the Eighteenth Amendment on individual States? Well if you want to drink excessively move to Nevada, Louisiana or Missouri.

Shit in the States of Louisiana and Missouri it's even legal to give alcohol to minors as long as it under adult supervision. In Missouri public intoxication is not only allowed local governments are prohibited from passing laws against it. In the State of Louisiana it's legal to have an open container in your automobile as long as it doesn't have a straw in it. On the other side of the spectrum, if you want to be clean and sober move to the State of Kansas. Even today there are still twenty nine counties that are completely dry. The Commonwealth of Pennsylvania stands out in that alcohol sales are completely controlled by the state. They own and operate all liquor businesses. All in all the Eighteenth Amendment to the United States Constitution was an incredible overreach of government power that failed miserably.

The Nineteenth Amendment to the United States Constitution

The text reads as such:

The right of citizens of the United States to vote shall not be denied or abridged by the United States or by any State on account of sex.

Congress shall have power to enforce this article by appropriate legislation.

Women's Suffrage: The Nineteenth Amendment to the United States Constitution is the legislation that FINALLY said "yes, if you have tits you can vote!" The Nineteenth Amendment was yet another citizenship right that rich, land owning, White men decided let the rest of American society enjoy. And it was long overdue. By the way, like it or not, the Nineteenth Amendment along with the Fourth, Ninth and Fourteenth Amendments give full, falsely denied, rights to all of those who belong to the LGBT community. However, its primary goal was to ensure voting equality to all American women.

Although woman's suffrage got its start in the United States in 1848 the gates to voting rights for women had its origins in the West. Specifically the State of Wyoming. When the Federal Government threatened to withhold statehood unless Wyoming rescinded voting rights for women state legislators let it be known that they would rather not be a part of the United States than take that right away from female citizens. While the concept of Manifest Destiny encouraged many Americans to establish settlements in the many western regions very few women went. It didn't take long for these Cowboys to realize that serial masturbation was not a long term thing. They concluded that "the lack of pussy is the root of all evil!" So the promise of voting rights was a great inducement for women to move west. Proving, once again, that a society without pussy will never survive itself. It will collapse like a black hole in the deepest parts of our universe. Once women arrived out west in sufficient numbers America's prominence in the world was guaranteed. This is an amazing example for future generations to learn. The State of Wyoming offered voting rights to women starting in 1850.

By the time the Nineteenth Amendment was passed women in Wyoming had quietly been exercising the right for seventy years! Other western states quickly followed suit as women's suffrage also had a significant economic impact on those communities that embraced any version of voting equality. The biggest being the increase in services providing mankind's three basic economic needs. Those being food, clothing and shelter. This, in turn, was a major factor in the boom that was the Industrial Revolution. So one could argue that America's economic might all lead back to a woman's honey pot. This book's predecessor, Three Blind Mice discusses in more detail life as a woman in the 1850s. However one part is worth mentioning again as it pertains to the Nineteenth Amendment. And that was the United States Supreme Court decision in Minor v Happersett (1875). In summary the Court ruled that woman don't have the right to vote in part because the Constitution specifically says "men!" This was akin to the 1896 United States Supreme Court decision in Plessy v Ferguson (1896) which introduced the idea of "separate but equal." Both of these court decisions were misguided, small minded and judicially stupid.

And surely contrary to the idea of "All men are created equal." The State of Wyoming would also be the first State in America to elect a female Governor. Her name was Nellie Tayloe Ross. She was an important symbol of the feminist movement in the 1920s. In addition to supporting the Nineteenth Amendment she was also a staunch Prohibitionist and supported the Eighteenth Amendment. Additionally, she supported the failed Child Labor Amendment that passed the United States House of Representatives and the United States Senate but failed to get state ratification. Of all of the brave women who fought for woman's suffrage none garnered more lasting fame than Susan B. Anthony. The Nineteenth Amendment is commonly known as the "Anthony Amendment." Susan B. Anthony was much more than a suffragette however. She was a teacher, author and civil rights activist. In addition to being a supporter of the right to vote, she also wanted women to own land, work and "be secure in their person" as promoted in the Fourth Amendment to the United States Constitution.

She would eventually be honored and have audience with Presidents William McKinley and Theodore Roosevelt. She would also be the only American woman to appear on United States currency. That would be the one dollar coin.

If you want an easy place to find them just get some change from a New York City subway vending machine. If Wyoming is at the front of American states when it comes to a woman's right to vote and the Nineteenth Amendment, the people of State of Tennessee would kick the winning field goal in this legislative Super Bowl. And the main Volunteer was a gentleman named Harry T.Burn. To become law the Nineteenth Amendment need to be ratified by thirty six of the forty eight states that made up the United States at the time (States forty nine and fifty, Alaska and Hawaii would not join the Union until 1959). By 1920 thirty five states had ratified the Amendment. In August 1920 the Tennessee Legislature had taken up the measure. Like much of the Southern United States at the time Tennessee was not only anti Black but anti suffrage and by default anti women as well. And the vote reflected these views as well. Mr. Burn was a Congressman in the Tennessee House of Representatives and had initially planned to vote against the measure. The vote was tied at forty eight apiece and Congressman Burn had the deciding vote.

At the last minute he would decide in favor of ratification and Tennessee would become the State that would guarantee America would finally eliminate voting discrimination based on gender. What changed his mind was a letter he received from his mother, Mrs. J.L. Burn of Niota, Tennessee. This is what she wrote:

Dear Son:

Hurrah and vote for suffrage! Don't keep them in doubt! I notice some of the speeches against. They were bitter. I have been watching to see how you stood, but have not noticed anything yet. Don't forget to be a good boy and help Mrs. Catt put the "rat" in ratification.

Your mother

Sweet, right? Goes to show not only the power of a mother, but also teaches the lesson that if you want to get shit done you can always look for a good mama's boy to do it. The "Mrs. Catt. referred to in the letter was Carrie Chapman Catt. The Iowa State University graduate was a firebrand and made a name for herself in the suffrage movement. She advocated aggressively and sometimes rubbed people the wrong way. She would be exposed as a racist later in life and this would temper her reputation.

The Twentieth Amendment to the United States Constitution:

The text reads as such:

Section 1. The terms of the President and Vice President shall end at noon on the 20th day of January, and the terms of Senators and Representatives at noon on the 3d day of January, of the years in which such terms would have ended if this article had not been ratified; and the terms of their successors shall then begin.

Section 2. The Congress shall assemble at least once in every year, and such meeting shall begin at noon on the 3d day of January, unless they shall by law appoint a different day.

Section 3. If, at the time fixed for the beginning of the term of the President, the President elect shall have died, the Vice President elect shall become President. If a President shall not have been chosen before the time fixed for the beginning of his term, or if the President elect shall have failed to qualify, then the Vice President elect shall act as President until a President shall have qualified; and the Congress may by law provide for the case wherein neither a President elect nor a Vice President elect shall have qualified, declaring who shall then act as President, or the manner in which one who is to act shall be selected, and such person shall act accordingly until a President or Vice President shall have qualified.

Section 4. The Congress may by law provide for the case of the death of any of the persons from whom the House of Representatives may choose a President whenever the right of choice shall have devolved upon them, and for the case of the death of any of the persons from whom the Senate may choose a Vice President whenever the right of choice shall have devolved upon them.

Section 5. Sections 1 and 2 shall take effect on the 15th day of October following the ratification of this article.

Section 6. This article shall be inoperative unless it shall have been ratified as an amendment to the Constitution by the legislatures of three-fourths of the several States within seven years from the date of its submission.

This is another redo on the process of electing the President and Vice President of the United States. The Twentieth Amendment also changes the effective date of when all federally elected officers go to work. The original date that the President and Vice President of the United States took office was March 4th following the election. The Twentieth Amendment moves the date up to January 20th. In the early Nineteenth Century transportation had yet to become mechanized. The introduction of the railroad would greatly change intra-city mobility. However, it still took a long fucking time to get around. So everyone had from November till March to get from wherever they lived (which, by 1850 stretched to California with her admission to the Union). Four months was plenty of time to get to Washington, D.C. With the advent of the Industrial Revolution, the Wright Brothers, Henry Ford, Howard Hughes, etc transportation changed dramatically. So it was now much easier to get to the nation's Capital in no time. Today, United States Congresspeople report on January 3rd and the President and Vice President of the United States start January 20th. Now every time there is a new President the Legislative Branch gets a two week jump to figure out how their gonna fuck over the Executive Branch. Even when the same party is in power.

There were political considerations in passing the Twentieth Amendment as well. Specifically, the American Civil War. After the election of 1860 the United States was politically caught between a rock and hard place. Abraham Lincoln's victory was the straw that broke the camel's back for the State of South Carolina. However he couldn't do anything about it. His predecessor, President James Buchanan "wouldn't" do anything about it. By March 4, 1863 Lincoln was all "Commander-In-Chief" and much less "President." He had to go to war immediately. Assuming he takes office in January maybe a diplomatic solution could have been accomplished. A lame duck United States Congress only had time to fester bad feelings between the North and the South. The other case was that of President William Henry Harrison. His inauguration speech was the longest of any President on one of the coldest wettest days (March 4th) of the year in 1841. Wearing no coat, no hat and riding on horseback versus carriage all combined to kill a month into his Presidency. He would die from pneumonia and set off yet another constitutional crises that wouldn't be fully rectified until the passage of the Twenty Fifth Amendment to the United States Constitution. The crucial question was whether or not Vice President John Tyler was Acting President of the United States or actual President. Fortunately, Mr. Tyler would settle the question and deciding he was actually President and get the fuck out of my face. Had President taken office on January 20, 1841 he almost assuredly would have dressed for the weather and served out his term. Franklin Roosevelt would be the first President to assume office on January 20 when he started his second term in 1937.

Chapter 10

❧

The Roosevelt Amendments, Twenty-One and Twenty-Two

The Twenty-First Amendment to the United States Constitution:

The text reads as such:

Section 1. The eighteenth article of amendment to the Constitution of the United States is hereby repealed.

Section 2. The transportation or importation into any State, Territory, or possession of the United States for delivery or use therein of intoxicating liquors, in violation of the laws thereof, is hereby prohibited.

Section 3. This article shall be inoperative unless it shall have been ratified as an amendment to the Constitution by conventions in the several States, as provided in the Constitution, within seven years from the date of the submission hereof to the States by the Congress.

The Twenty-First Amendment repealed the Eighteenth Amendment to the United States Constitution. Basically, this is the United States Government admitting to its citizens that they shit the bed on banning alcohol. They said, "Yes, we know we fucked up. We thought we were smarter than Jesus. We forgot he turned wine into water!" For punishment, God gave America a decade of crime, murder, lawlessness and a severe degradation of society. So the Twenty-First Amendment is the Government's apology to God. Oh, yeah, for shits and giggles he threw in a stock market crash and a great depression to make sure they didn't forget not to fuck with a man's booze. Its passage was greatly influenced by the Democratic Presidential Candidate Franklin Roosevelt.

As mentioned earlier among many promises Candidate Roosevelt made during the election campaign of 1932 was a "wet" platform. His intention was to support all legislation that repealed Prohibition. This combined with the meteoric rise of organized crime moved the nation to repeal the Eighteenth Amendment. The breakdown of the Amend goes like this: The first section of the Twenty-First Amendment repeals the Eighteenth, period. The second section basically gives regulation of alcohol to the States. As a result, the what and where you purchase and consume liquor varies wildly from state to state. The third section sets a seven year sunset for the States to ratify the legislation. South Carolina was the only State to vote against ratification. The Twenty-First Amendment to the United States Constitution was adopted on December 5th, 1933.

The Twenty-Second Amendment to the United States Constitution:

The text reads as such:

Section 1. No person shall be elected to the office of the President more than twice, and no person who has held the office of President, or acted as President, for more than two years of a term to which some other person was elected President shall be elected to the office of the President more than once. But this article shall not apply to any person holding the office of President when this article was proposed by the Congress, and shall not prevent any person who may be holding the office of President, or acting as President, during the term within which this article becomes operative from holding the office of President or acting as President during the remainder of such term.

Section 2. This article shall be inoperative unless it shall have been ratified as an amendment to the Constitution by the legislatures of three-fourths of the several states within seven years from the date of its submission to the states by the Congress.

The Twenty-Second Amendment simply sets term limits on how long a person can serve as President of the United States. You get a flat eight years, that's it. The impetus for the measure was directly related to President Franklin Roosevelt serving four terms. It was just too fucking long. After winning the 1932 Presidential Election he was basically "President for Life." Just like Josef Stalin, Pol Pot, Hugo Chavez, Yasser Arafat, Benito Mussolini and Adolf Hitler. So, the Twenty-Second Amendment says, "Oh no, we ain't lettin' that shit happen again!" And while we're at it let's dispel this honorable notion of George Washington setting a precedent of voluntarily relinquishing power after two terms as the complete truth about the man. He was tired after all of the shit he had done up until that point in his life. A quick review: He commanded a regiment on the front end of the French and Indian War in 1754 (it was his failures here that would make him such an effective General during the American Revolutionary War). During the War for American independence he not only led, he managed, organized and commanded an under-armed and under-manned group of like minded men to victory. THEN, he help set up a whole fucking country! After that he said, "Ok, I'll run the motherfucka for ya too.

But only for eight years, shit. I'm tired already." Joking aside President Washington was greatly influenced by Cincinnatus. The irony being Cincinnatus voluntarily gave up power two weeks later on the other hand. George Washington was enchanted by the idea of voluntarily giving up power just like Cincinnatus had. Proponents of the Twenty Second Amendment like to cite George Washington as setting an unwritten rule about two terms. So, Franklin Roosevelt's' FOUR terms was just too much. Shit, it killed him. The Twenty-Second Amendment did have the support of President Harry S. Truman. Why wouldn't he be? It didn't affect him at all. The Amendment was passed by the United States Congress in 1947. It was ratified by the requisite number of States by 1951.

Chapter 11

❧

The Civil Rights Amendments, Twenty Three and Twenty Four

The Twenty-Third and Twenty-Fourth Amendments to the United States Constitution are known as the "Civil Rights Amendments." The distinction between term "Civil Rights Amendments" and "Reconstruction Amendments" is unique in its definition. The Thirteenth, Fourteenth and Fifteenth Amendments specifically addressed civil rights. The Twenty-Third and Twenty-Fourth Amendments relate to voting rights. Two other things happened as well. One, they were both passed during the Kennedy Administration. And two, both the Kennedy Administration and the Democratic Party both benefited from the passage and ratification of the Amendments. Both Amendments greatly benefited Blacks in the United States. Black people had, by now, deeply and on a massive scale, moved their voting allegiance to the Democrat party. Especially in the southern part of the nation. Since both Amendments dealt with citizen's rights and elections, by default the Democratic Party was and remains the main benefactors of these measures.

Along with the Reconstruction Amendments the Twenty-Third and Twenty Fourth Amendments make up the "African American Bill of Rights." For Black folks these five Amendments validate the rest of the United States Constitution. Washington, D.C. is one of the blackest cities in America and the Twenty-Fourth's ending of the poll taxes was directed getting Black folks the vote.

The Twenty-Third Amendment to the United States Constitution

The text reads as such:

Section 1. The District constituting the seat of Government of the United States shall appoint in such manner as the Congress may direct:

A number of electors of President and Vice President equal to the whole number of Senators and Representatives in Congress to which the District would be entitled if it were a State, but in no event more than the least populous State; they shall be in addition to those appointed by the States, but they shall be considered, for the purposes of the election of President and Vice President, to be electors appointed by a State; and they shall meet in the District and perform such duties as provided by the twelfth article of amendment.

Section 2. The Congress shall have power to enforce this article by appropriate legislation.

The Twenty-Third Amendment officially gives the residents of Washington, D.C. "some" form of representation in the voting process for national office specifically the President and Vice President of the United States. So, although resident license plates sport the motto "no taxation without representation" this is not entirely true. It don't mean it's entirely false either. There are no United States Congresspersons representing Washington, D.C. But, that said there is no one representing any other city either. But the Federal District is a different entity than any other city in the United States. It was set up to be the corporate office of the United States Federal Government. The Founding Fathers never meant it to be a living city; it was suppose to strictly be an administrative location. But people being people they're gonna live whenever they can. And yes, eventually they're gonna want voting rights. Anyway, the Republican Party knew that offering Electoral College votes to the residents of the city would mean giving Democrats three Electoral votes in perpetuity. Since then the Democratic Party has gone into every Presidential Election knowing they come out the box with those votes in hand. It's like a boxer already having a round in his bag before the fight ever starts.

And remember, the number of Electoral College votes is the name of the game in Presidential politics. The count currently stands at two hundred seventy one for the big prize. In many ways the Twenty-Third Amendment was blow to statehood and Congressional representation. Also, there are those that argue if all the fuss from Washington D.C. residents is about representation in the United States Congress then they should be given "voting" citizenship in the State of Maryland (who conceded the land that is the District today). Only problem is Maryland don't want D.C. in any form. Wonder why. Hmmm. The Twenty-Third Amendment to the United States Constitution was ratified by the requisite number of states in March, 1961.

The Twenty-Fourth Amendment to the United States Constitution:

The text reads as such:

Section 1. The right of citizens of the United States to vote in any primary or other election for President or Vice President, for electors for President or Vice President, or for Senator or Representative in Congress, shall not be denied or abridged by the United States or any State by reason of failure to pay any poll tax or other tax.

Section 2. The Congress shall have power to enforce this article by appropriate legislation.

The Twenty-Fourth Amendment eliminated poll taxes as it related to Federal elections. The important word here is "Federal." It's important because it didn't eliminate the practice at the State and Local level. It had the support of the Kennedy Administration and the Democratic Party because they stood to benefit from its passage.

Passed in the United States Congress during the Kennedy Administration and ratified a majority of the states while Lyndon B. Johnson was President it was another piece to the "Black folks want the same fucking citizen rights as everybody fucking else" playbook. The Twenty-Fourth Amendment is the sister Amendment to the Fifteenth Amendment which granted voting right without regard to race (meaning Black folks). All of this beside the fact that it was just the right fucking thing to do. The history of poll taxes is a great place to start the discussion. And to have that discussion you have to go back to the end of the American Civil War. While politically Reconstruction started with the passage of the Thirteenth Amendment it enraged the elitist in the Southern United States. They hated the new "uppity" citizenship of former slaves. They cared more about this repercussion of the Civil War more than their own personal losses. Reconstruction and the passage of the Fifteenth Amendment not gave Blacks the vote but also put Blacks in office all across the South and Washington, D.C. From the heights of state government to the United States Congress former slaves got a voice in America.

So the Reconstruction Era would be about a struggle of Black voting rights and certain Whites to retarding those rights. This would lead to, among other things, the creation of the Ku Klux Klan. They didn't hate Black folks half as much as they hated Black folks with the right to vote. It was too fucking many of them by the end of the Civil War. Poll taxes were the side effect of the rolling back of Reconstruction initiatives that came with the election of Rutherford B. Hayes in 1877. President Hayes was one of four Presidents who won the Electoral College but lost the popular vote. The compromise was he would be given the top spot on the condition he would end Reconstruction. He said. "Fuck yeah." While Hayes supported full citizenship for all he also wanted to be President of the United States. So he made a deal with the Devil to become President of the United States. Not long after taking office he pulled all Federal troops from the South leaving them to govern on their own. Meaning that the pre-Civil War powerful were back in play. One of the first pay-back items was restricting the vote. Along with intimidation, poll taxes were very effective. Regarding poll taxes here were a whole of new rules put in place to keep Southern Blacks from voting.

While they varied from state to state they were basically all the same. If you're Black, you gotta pay to vote. If you're White, well, welcome. Some states combined these poll taxes with literacy tests whose requirements were unevenly applied. The Twenty-Fourth Amendment erased this requirement. The loophole in the legislation was that it only applied to Federal elections. This allowed certain states to manipulate the measure under "states rights" declarations. The defining United States Supreme Court case would be Harper v Virginia State Board of Elections (1966). Here the court ruled that the Twenty-Fourth Amendment applied to all elections regardless of level. However, Southern racists had a good ninety year run. Annie Harper was a Black woman who sued for the right to vote without paying for the privilege. Brilliantly her attorneys argued not from a "citizen's rights" point of view but from a "citizenship" point of view. They used the Fourteenth Amendment to the United States Constitution and the Equal Protection Clause to make their case. The shit worked too. Now voting is free, as it should be. The Twenty-Fourth Amendment to the United States Constitution was ratified on January 23rd, 1964.

The only state to specifically reject the Amendment was the State of Mississippi. Additionally the following states have never ratified the Amendment:

1. State of Arizona
2. State of Arkansas
3. State of Georgia
4. State of Louisiana
5. State of Mississippi
6. State of Oklahoma

7. State of South Carolina
8. State of Wyoming

Of these states the State of Wyoming stands out because they hold such a leading role in voting rights historically.

Chapter 12

❧

The Oswald Amendment, The Twenty-Fifth Amendment to the United States Constitution

The Twenty-Fifth Amendment to the United States Constitution

The text reads as such:

Section 1. In case of the removal of the President from office or of his death or resignation, the Vice President shall become President.

Section 2. Whenever there is a vacancy in the office of the Vice President, the President shall nominate a Vice President who shall take office upon confirmation by a majority vote of both Houses of Congress.

Section 3. Whenever the President transmits to the President pro tempore of the Senate and the Speaker of the House of Representatives his written declaration that he is unable to discharge the powers and duties of his office, and until he transmits to them a written declaration to the contrary, such powers and duties shall be discharged by the Vice President as Acting President.

Section 4. Whenever the Vice President and a majority of either the principal officers of the executive departments or of such other body as Congress may by law provide, transmit to the President pro tempore of the Senate and the Speaker of the House of Representatives their written declaration that the President is unable to discharge the powers and duties of his office, the Vice President shall immediately assume the powers and duties of the office as Acting President.

Thereafter, when the President transmits to the President pro tempore of the Senate and the Speaker of the House of Representatives his written declaration that no inability exists, he shall resume the powers and duties of his office unless the Vice President and a majority of either the principal officers of the executive department or of such other body as Congress may by law provide, transmit within four days to the President pro tempore of the Senate and the Speaker of the House of Representatives their written declaration that the President is unable to discharge the powers and duties of his office. Thereupon Congress shall decide the issue, assembling within forty-eight hours for that purpose if not in session. If the Congress, within twenty-one days after receipt of the latter written declaration, or, if Congress is not in session, within twenty-one days after Congress is required to assemble, determines by two-thirds vote of both Houses that the President is unable to discharge the powers and duties of his office, the Vice President shall continue to discharge the same as Acting President; otherwise, the President shall resume the powers and duties of his office.

The Twenty-Fifth Amendment is so named the "Oswald Amendment" because it addressed Presidential succession questions recently raised following the assassination of President John F. Kennedy. Politically, after the assassination of President John F. Kennedy the Presidential line of succession was grim at best. Vice President Lyndon B. Johnson was sixty four years old and had already had a heart attack. Next in the Presidential line of succession was John McCormack. Representative McCormack, of the Commonwealth of Massachusetts was Speaker of the House starting in the second session of the Eighty-Seventh United States Congress. HE was seventy one years old. Next in line was United States Senator Carl Hayden also serving as the Senate Pro Tempore. From the State of Arizona Senator Hayden was eighty-six year old. So in very short order there could have been chaos at the highest levels of the United States Government. As it was, on paper, it was "pausing." The moral of the story is that something had to be done to address these issues. So, if Lee Harvey Oswald doesn't kill (alone?) President John F. Kennedy it's doubtful that the Twenty-Fifth Amendment is ever drafted, let alone, enacted. In addition addressing the Presidential line of succession the real "mousetrap" of the Twenty-Fifth Amendment is Section Four of the text. Section Four basically says that if the Vice President of the United States and a few of his homies decide so they can kick the President of the United States out of office and take this motherfucker over. Section Four of the Twenty-Fifth Amendment is nothing more than a blueprint for staging a coup d'état, American style. Here is the scenario:

The Vice President of the United States and the Cabinet decide that the President of the United States has, all of a sudden, become an asshole and he has to go.

All they have to do is submit a letter to the Speaker of the United States House of Representatives and the Senate Pro Tempore of the United States Senate and "viola," he is Acting President of the United States. That's it! It's that fucking easy. Now, of course the sitting President of the United States can just as easily send a letter to the same to people in the Legislative Branch saying the Vice President and the Cabinet is full of shit and I ain't going nowhere. The Vice President can send a SECOND letter and say the same shit he said the first time and he's right back in the Oval Office of the White House until the United States Congress decides which of these motherfuckers is truly crazy. A simple two-thirds majority vote will decide the matter. There are two problems here. First, Section Four is waaayyy too easy to manipulate if certain parties were intent on doing so. Second, Twenty-First Century politics combined with a twenty-four news cycle mixed in with the blinding speed of social media makes the impact of such a scenario almost immediate, and not in a good way. Global financial markets would almost certainly sell off the minute the news became public. Additionally, special interest groups, both domestic and international would take sides and try to influence the electorate to their guy. Even after Congress decides who really is President of the United States, ill feelings will still linger for some time after. An even scarier notion is the Vice President of the United States doesn't even need the Cabinet to back his play. Section Four also says that the Vice President and "other such body as Congress may provide by law" can submit a letter. Well, shit, that can mean any fucking body. The United States Congress can commission the local chapter of the International Brotherhood of Electrical Workers (IBEW) to be that designated body.

Your kid's high school chess club or a church choir could do the job based on the legislation. None of these scenarios are probable but they are definitely plausible. This is what makes the Twenty-Fifth Amendment a bit shaky as an Amendment. Section Four is only one part of the overall issue of succession. The history of the Amendment can trace itself back to three other events besides the assassination of President John F. Kennedy. One was Vice President John Tyler and the death of President William Henry Harrison. The second was a severe thrombotic stroke suffered by President Woodrow Wilson during his second term. The third was the Presidential Act of 1947. As discussed earlier in the book, after President Harrison had died there was some question whether or not Vice President John Tyler was "President" or "Acting President." Well he settled the issue when he simply said to everybody, "fuck you, I'm the Man, not the Acting Man!" Everyone was like, "damn, ok brotha!" Things were a little different after the death of President Franklin D. Roosevelt. Among many things, politically, that occurred one of those was the Presidential Act of 1947. Now President Wilson? If nothing motivated the passage of the Twenty-Fifth Amendment it was the events that happened after he had his stroke. His second wife, Edith Galt, in collusion with the President's doctors managed to keep the nation in the dark for four months about how really fucked up that stroke left him. From October 1919 to February 1920 they lied, cajoled and intimidated the entire Administration. At the top of the "to be bullshitted list was Vice President Thomas Marshall. When the shit became public he was urged to declare himself Acting President of the United States. But he pussed out and refused to go all "John Tyler" on their ass. As a result of this Edith Galt is popularly known as the America's first female President of the United States by most historians.

The basic tenant of the 1947 Act was to change the line of succession at the time, after the Vice President of the United States, from the Senate Pro Tempore to the Speaker of the United States House of

Representatives. For President Harry S. Truman part of his support for the legislation was the fact that him and then House Speaker Sam Rayburn was very tight homies. President Truman and Speaker Rayburn was fast drinking buddies. Shit, he was throwing back bourbons from the Commonwealth of Kentucky when he found out he was the MAN after President Roosevelt had died. Added to that was the other fact that he could give a shit about then Senate Pro Tempore Senator Kenneth McKellar. So this was a direct "fuck you" to him as well. President Truman figured he be damned before he'd see that son of a bitch running the country. Because of the Twenty-Fifth Amendment we currently have the following Presidential line of succession:

1. Vice President of the United States
2. Speaker of the United States House of Representatives
3. Senate Pro Tempore of the United States Senate
4. United States Secretary of State
5. United States Secretary of the Treasury
6. United States Secretary of Defense
7. Attorney General of the United States
8. United States Secretary of the Interior
9. United States Secretary of Agriculture
10. United States Secretary of Commerce
11. United States Secretary of Labor
12. United States Secretary of Health and Human Services
13. United States Secretary of Housing and Urban Development
14. United States Secretary of Transportation
15. United States Secretary of Education
16. United States Secretary of Veterans Affairs
17. United States Secretary of Homeland Security

The problem with the Presidential line of succession has always been the placement of the United States Senate Pro Tempore. Typically this is not so much an "elected" position as it is an appointed. This leadership position is usually reserved for the most senior member of the United States Senate. Meaning, longest serving. This also means the oldest United Senator in the governing body.

For this person to even be in the line of succession is a bit out of whack. Typically this guy is waaayy too old to be in the United States Senate much less being President of the United States. The Twenty-Fifth Amendment to the United States Constitution was ratified on February 23, 1967. The State of Nebraska was the first to ratify.

Chapter 13

❦

The Kids Get The Vote And Congress Gets Paid, The Twenty-Sixth and Twenty Seventh Amendments to the United States Constitution

The Twenty-Six Amendment to the United States Constitution

The text reads as such:

Section 1. The right of citizens of the United States, who are eighteen years of age or older, to vote shall not be denied or abridged by the United States or by any State on account of age.

Section 2. The Congress shall have the power to enforce this article by appropriate legislation.

The Twenty-Six Amendment guarantees the vote to the kids. By kids I mean eighteen year olds. The Old Heads finally figured out two things.

One, that if the boys are old enough to jerk off and get asses shot off in Vietnam they're old enough to vote. And two, the girls were already 18 in intellect when they turned fourteen! So this realization brought enough folks to the obvious table to get this done.

Gender suffrage was first mentioned in 1954 by President Dwight D. Eisenhower in his State of the Union Address that year. Along with the Fifteenth and Nineteenth Amendments they are collectively known as the "Suffrage Amendments." The Fifteenth Amendment addressed racial suffrage. The Nineteenth addressed gender suffrage. The Twenty-Sixth became necessary after the United States Supreme Court ruled an extension to the Voting Rights Act of 1965 unconstitutional. It basically said the same shit. The Twenty-Sixth also unified voting rights for the young at every election level. Federal, State and Local. Most states had widely varying age requirements as to who can vote and who can't. The war in Vietnam War was also a factor in the voting age being established. The right to fight was a lot more appealing for patriotic sales package the Federal Government was selling to its citizens. And it worked too. The 1972 Presidential Election saw a fifty five percent turnout. Alas, like all things with young people the novelty of the new toy wore off. By 1988 voter turnout among young adults had fallen off to thirty six percent. The Amendment was passed by the Ninety-Second United States Congress. This was a wartime Congress and many issues were on the legislative agenda. Including:

The passage of Title Nine

District of Columbia Voting Rights Amendment (among the six that didn't make the cut). The Amendment was ratified in 1971.

The Twenty-Seventh Amendment to the United States Constitution

The text reads as such:

No law, varying the compensation for the services of the Senators and Representatives, shall take effect, until an election of Representatives shall have intervened.

The Twenty-Seventh Amendment to the United States Constitution basically says that the United States Congress can't vote a pay raise for each other and get paid immediately. The Twenty-Seventh Amendment is also unique in that it was submitted to the States on September 25, 1789. It wouldn't be ratified by the requisite number of states until May 7, 1992! This represents a span of two hundred two years and change. This Amendment was initially part of the original United States Bill of Rights. It was submitted as a list of twelve by then United States Congressman James Madison. So, of the original twelve Amendments to the United States Constitution ten were ratified as the United States Bill of Rights, one became the Twenty-Seventh Amendment and the remaining Amendment, the Congressional Apportionment Amendment is, technically still pending as one of the six Amendments that didn't make the cut. Crazy shit to say the least. Back to the Twenty Seventh Amendment. Historically compensation of United States of United States Congressmen (I say "Congressmen" because the first woman didn't serve until 1916) was always shitty. This was the same way to make power only available to the few who could afford it (following the States' model).

It's a brilliant fucking move if you're a white, land owning male in the Nineteenth Century. The history of Congressional compensation has varied over the country's history. In 1789 Senators were paid six days per day. Today Congresspeople are paid one hundred seventy four thousand dollars per year (and still bitching about it ain't enough). The biggest percentage increase was in 1855 when salaries went to three thousand dollars per year. A one hundred percent increase. Salaries actually decreased during the World Wars and the Great Depression. Since the 1980s leadership in both chambers of the United States Congress receives slightly higher compensation that all others. Today that number is closer to three hundred thousand dollars. The other notable figure in the history of the Twenty-seventh Amendment is a gentleman named Gregory Watson. Mr. Watson was a student at the University of Texas at Austin. He wrote a class term paper on the fact that the Twenty-Seventh Amendment to the United States Constitution had not been ratified. Eventually the paper would reach the attention of many State legislatures. Ten years later in May 1992 the Amendment would be ratified. Funny shit is he got a C on the paper. His teacher was a woman named Sharon Waite. She said that his thesis was "unlikely and irrelevant." This turned out to be more a reflection on her limitations than on Mr. Watson's. This is precisely why what is possible is truly within ourselves when we so choose. He would become known as the "Stepfather of the Twenty-Seventh Amendment." The Twenty-Seventh Amendment also was possible by a United States Supreme ruling in Coleman v. Miller, 1939. In the case the Court ruled that where Amendments to the United States Constitution were concerned, if there was no sunset date attached to it ratification by the States then that legislation would be in a pending status in perpetuity. Meaning that at any time ratification was possible.

This is what allowed the Twenty-Seventh Amendment to finally achieve ratification two hundred plus years later. I will reiterate that of the six Amendments that passed the United States House of Representatives and the United States Senate but failed to get state ratification, four of them are technically still pending in "perpetuity" since they have no deadline for state ratification attached to them. They include the:

Congressional Apportionment Amendment
Title of Nobility Amendment
Corwin Amendment
Child Labor Agreement

Each of these Amendments can be added to the Twenty-First Century version of the United States Constitution by the requisite thirty eights states ratifying them. The most disturbing of these pending Amendments is the Corwin Amendment. It basically says that Black folks can be legislated as slaves again forever. Yea, most will argue that the Thirteenth Amendment would make passage a moot point but even the symbolism of the possibility is a stain on the Constitutional Process.

Chapter 14

❧

The Articles of Confederation, The United States Constitution, The Universal Declaration Of Human Rights and the Magna Carta

So, the United States Constitution is made up of the originally text (seven articles) and the twenty seven additional amendments. When it's all said and done the Constitution came into being like anything else in life. Money.

The original Articles of Confederation was a wordy, legal piece of shit.

The text reads as such:

To all to whom these Presents shall come, we the undersigned Delegates of the States affixed to our Names send greeting.

Articles of Confederation and perpetual Union between the states of New Hampshire, Massachusetts-bay Rhode Island and Providence Plantations, Connecticut, New York, New Jersey, Pennsylvania, Delaware, Maryland, Virginia, North Carolina, South Carolina and Georgia.

I.

The Stile of this Confederacy shall be

"The United States of America".

II.

Each state retains its sovereignty, freedom, and independence, and every power, jurisdiction, and right, which is not by this Confederation expressly delegated to the United States, in Congress assembled.

III.

The said States hereby severally enter into a firm league of friendship with each other, for their common defense, the security of their liberties, and their mutual and general welfare, binding themselves to assist each other, against all force offered to, or attacks made upon them, or any of them, on account of religion, sovereignty, trade, or any other pretense whatever.

IV.

The better to secure and perpetuate mutual friendship and intercourse among the people of the different States in this Union, the free inhabitants of each of these States, paupers, vagabonds, and fugitives from justice excepted, shall be entitled to all privileges and immunities of free citizens in the several States; and the people of each State shall free ingress and regress to and from any other State, and shall enjoy therein all the

privileges of trade and commerce, subject to the same duties, imposi-
tions, and restrictions as the inhabitants thereof respectively, provided
that such restrictions shall not extend so far as to prevent the removal of
property imported into any State, to any other State, of which the owner
is an inhabitant; provided also that no imposition, duties or restriction
shall be laid by any State, on the property of the United States, or either
of them.

If any person guilty of, or charged with, treason, felony, or other
high misdemeanor in any State, shall flee from justice, and be found in
any of the United States, he shall, upon demand of the Governor or
executive power of the State from which he fled, be delivered up and
removed to the State having jurisdiction of his offense.

Full faith and credit shall be given in each of these States to the
records, acts, and judicial proceedings of the courts and magistrates of
every other State.

V.

For the most convenient management of the general interests of the
United States, delegates shall be annually appointed in such manner as
the legislatures of each State shall direct, to meet in Congress on the first
Monday in November, in every year, with a powerreserved to each State
to recall its delegates, or any of them, at any time within the year, and to
send others in their stead for the remainder of the year.

No State shall be represented in Congress by less than two, nor more
than seven members; and no person shall be capable of being a delegate
for more than three years in any term of six years; nor shall any person,

being a delegate, be capable of holding any office under the United States, for which he, or another for his benefit, receives any salary, fees or emolument of any kind.

Each State shall maintain its own delegates in a meeting of the States, and while they act as members of the committee of the States.

In determining questions in the United States in Congress assembled, each State shall have one vote.

Freedom of speech and debate in Congress shall not be impeached or questioned in any court or place out of Congress, and the members of Congress shall be protected in their persons from arrests or imprisonments, during the time of their going to and from, and attendence on Congress, except for treason, felony, or breach of the peace.

VI.

No State, without the consent of the United States in Congress assembled, shall send any embassy to, or receive any embassy from, or enter into any conference, agreement, alliance or treaty with any King, Prince or State; nor shall any person holding any office of profit or trust under the United States, or any of them, accept any present, emolument, office or title of any kind whatever from any King, Prince or foreign State; nor shall the United States in Congress assembled, or any of them, grant any title of nobility.

No two or more States shall enter into any treaty, confederation or alliance whatever between them, without the consent of the United States in Congress assembled, specifying accurately the purposes for which the same is to be entered into, and how long it shall continue.

No State shall lay any imposts or duties, which may interfere with any stipulations in treaties, entered into by the United States in Congress assembled, with any King, Prince or State, in pursuance of any treaties already proposed by Congress, to the courts of France and Spain.

No vessel of war shall be kept up in time of peace by any State, except such number only, as shall be deemed necessary by the United States in Congress assembled, for the defense of such State, or its trade; nor shall any body of forces be kept up by any State in time of peace, except such number only, as in the judgement of the United States in Congress assembled, shall be deemed requisite to garrison the forts necessary for the defense of such State; but every State shall always keep up a well-regulated and disciplined militia, sufficiently armed and accoutered, and shall provide and constantly have ready for use, in public stores, a due number of filed pieces and tents, and a proper quantity of arms, ammunition and camp equipage.

No State shall engage in any war without the consent of the United States in Congress assembled, unless such State be actually invaded by enemies, or shall have received certain advice of a resolution being formed by some nation of Indians to invade such State, and the danger is so imminent as not to admit of a delay till the United States in Congress assembled can be consulted; nor shall any State grant commissions to any ships or vessels of war, nor letters of marque or reprisal, except it be after a declaration of war by the United States in Congress assembled, and then only against the Kingdom or State and the subjects thereof, against which war has been so declared, and under such regulations as shall be established by the United States in Congress assembled, unless such State be infested by pirates, in which case vessels of war may be fitted out for that occasion, and kept so long as the danger shall continue, or until the United States in Congress assembled shall determine otherwise.

VII.

When land forces are raised by any State for the common defense, all officers of or under the rank of colonel, shall be appointed by the legislature of each State respectively, by whom such forces shall be raised, or in such manner as such State shall direct, and all vacancies shall be filled up by the State which first made the appointment.

VIII.

All charges of war, and all other expenses that shall be incurred for the common defense or general welfare, and allowed by the United States in Congress assembled, shall be defrayed out of a common treasury, which shall be supplied by the several States in proportion to the value of all land within each State, granted or surveyed for any person, as such land and the buildings and improvements thereon shall be estimated according to such mode as the United States in Congress assembled, shall from time to time direct and appoint.

The taxes for paying that proportion shall be laid and levied by the authority and direction of the legislatures of the several States within the time agreed upon by the United States in Congress assembled.

IX.

The United States in Congress assembled, shall have the sole and exclusive right and power of determining on peace and war, except in the cases mentioned in the sixth article -- of sending and receiving ambassadors -- entering into treaties and alliances, provided that no treaty of commerce shall be made whereby the legislative power of the respective States shall be restrained from imposing such imposts and duties on foreigners, as their own people are subjected to, or from prohibiting the exportation or importation of any species of goods or commodities whatsoever -- of establishing rules for deciding in all cases, what captures on land or water shall be legal, and in what manner prizes taken by land or naval forces in the service of the United States shall be divided or appropriated -- of granting letters of marque and reprisal in times of peace -- appointing courts for the trial of piracies and felonies commited on the high seas and establishing courts for receiving and determining finally appeals in all cases of captures, provided that no member of Congress shall be appointed a judge of any of the said courts.

The United States in Congress assembled shall also be the last resort on appeal in all disputes and differences now subsisting or that hereafter may arise between two or more States concerning boundary, jurisdiction or any other causes whatever; which authority shall always be exercised in the manner following. Whenever the legislative or executive authority or lawful agent of any State in controversy with another shall present a petition to Congress stating the matter in question and praying for a hearing, notice thereof shall be given by order of Congress to the legislative or executive authority of the other State in controversy, and a day assigned for the appearance of the parties by their lawful agents, who shall then be directed to appoint by joint consent, commissioners or judges to constitute a court for hearing and determining the matter in question: but if they cannot agree, Congress shall name three persons out of each of the United States, and from the list of such persons each party shall alternately strike out one, the petitioners beginning, until the number shall be reduced to thirteen; and from that number not less than seven, nor more than nine names as Congress shall direct, shall in the presence of Congress be drawn out by lot, and the persons whose names shall be so drawn or any five of them, shall be commissioners or judges, to hear and finally determine the controversy, so always as a major part of the judges who shall hear the cause shall agree in the determination: and if either party shall neglect to attend at the day appointed, without showing reasons, which Congress shall judge sufficient, or being present shall refuse to strike, the Congress shall proceed to nominate three persons out of each State, and the secretary of Congress shall strike in behalf of such party absent or refusing; and the judgement and sentence of the court to be appointed, in the manner before prescribed, shall be final and conclusive; and if any of the parties shall refuse to submit to the authority of such court, or to appear or defend their claim or cause, the court shall nevertheless proceed to pronounce sentence, or judgement, which shall in like manner be final and decisive, the judgement or sentence and other proceedings being in either case transmitted to Congress, and lodged among the acts of Congress for the security of the parties concerned: provided that every commissioner, before he sits in judgement, shall take an oath to be administered by one of the judges of the supreme or superior court of the State, where the cause shall be tried, 'well and truly to hear and determine the matter in question, according to the best of his judgement, without favor, affection or hope of reward': provided also, that no State shall be deprived of territory for the benefit of the United States.

All controversies concerning the private right of soil claimed under different grants of two or more States, whose jurisdictions as they may respect such lands, and the States which passed such grants are adjusted, the said grants or either of them being at the same time claimed to have originated antecedent to such settlement of jurisdiction, shall on the petition of either party to the Congress of the United States, be finally determined as near as may be in the same manner as is before prescribed for deciding disputes respecting territorial jurisdiction between different States.

The United States in Congress assembled shall also have the sole and exclusive right and power of regulating the alloy and value of coin struck by their own authority, or by that of the respective States -- fixing the standards of weights and measures throughout the United States -- regulating the trade and managing all affairs with the Indians, not members of any of the States, provided that the legislative right of any State within its own limits be not infringed or violated -- establishing or regulating post offices from one State to another, throughout all the United States, and exacting such postage on the papers passing through the same as may be requisite to defray the expenses of the said office -- appointing all officers of the land forces, in the service of the United States, excepting regimental officers -- appointing all the officers of the naval forces, and commissioning all officers whatever in the service of the United States -- making rules for the government and regulation of the said land and naval forces, and directing their operations.

The United States in Congress assembled shall have authority to appoint a committee, to sit in the recess of Congress, to be denominated 'A Committee of the States', and to consist of one delegate from each State; and to appoint such other committees and civil officers as may be necessary for managing the general affairs of the United States under their direction -- to appoint one of their members to preside, provided that no person be allowed to serve in the office of president more than one year in any term of three years; to ascertain the necessary sums of money to be raised for the service of the United States, and to appropriate and apply the same for defraying the public expenses -- to borrow money, or emit bills on the credit of the United States, transmitting every half-year to the respective States an account of the sums of money so borrowed or emitted -- to build and equip a navy -- to agree upon the number of land forces, and to make requisitions from each State for its quota, in proportion to the number of white inhabitants in such State; which requisition shall be binding, and thereupon the legislature of each State shall appoint the regimental officers, raise the men and cloath, arm and equip them in a solid-like manner, at the expense of the United States; and the officers and men so cloathed, armed and equipped shall march to the place appointed, and within the time agreed on by the United States in Congress assembled. But if the United States in Congress assembled shall, on consideration of circumstances judge proper that any State should not raise men, or should raise a smaller number of men than the quota thereof, such extra number shall be raised, officered, cloathed, armed and equipped in the same manner as the quota of each State, unless the legislature of such State shall judge that such extra number cannot be safely spread out in the same, in which case they shall raise, officer, cloath, arm and equip as many of such extra number as they judeg can be safely spared. And the officers and men so cloathed, armed, and equipped, shall march to the place appointed, and within the time agreed on by the United States in Congress assembled.

The United States in Congress assembled shall never engage in a war, nor grant letters of marque or reprisal in time of peace, nor enter into any treaties or alliances, nor coin money, nor regulate the value thereof, nor ascertain the sums and expenses necessary for the defense and welfare of the United States, or any of them, nor emit bills, nor borrow money on the credit of the United States, nor appropriate money, nor agree upon the number of vessels of war, to be built or purchased, or the number of land or sea forces to be raised, nor appoint a commander in chief of the army or navy, unless nine States assent to the same: nor shall a question on any other point, except for adjourning from day to day be determined, unless by the votes of the majority of the United States in Congress assembled.

The Congress of the United States shall have power to adjourn to any time within the year, and to any place within the United States, so that no period of adjournment be for a longer duration than the space of six months, and shall publish the journal of their proceedings monthly, except such parts thereof relating to treaties, alliances or military operations, as in their judgement require secrecy; and the yeas and nays of the delegates of each State on any question shall be entered on the journal, when it is desired by any delegates of a State, or any of them, at his or their request shall be furnished with a transcript of the said journal, except such parts as are above excepted, to lay before the legislatures of the several States.

X.

The Committee of the States, or any nine of them, shall be authorized to execute, in the recess of Congress, such of the powers of Congress as the United States in Congress assembled, by the consent of the nine States, shall from time to time think expedient to vest them with; provided that no power be delegated to the said Committee, for the exercise of which, by the Articles of Confederation, the voice of nine States in the Congress of the United States assembled be requisite.

XI.

Canada acceding to this confederation, and adjoining in the measures of the United States, shall be admitted into, and entitled to all the advantages of this Union; but no other colony shall be admitted into the same, unless such admission be agreed to by nine States.

XII.

All bills of credit emitted, monies borrowed, and debts contracted by, or under the authority of Congress, before the assembling of the United States, in pursuance of the present confederation, shall be deemed and considered as a charge against the United States, for payment and satisfaction whereof the said United States, and the public faith are hereby solemnly pleged.

XIII.

Every State shall abide by the determination of the United States in Congress assembled, on all questions which by this confederation are submitted to them. And the Articles of this Confederation shall be inviolably observed by every State, and the Union shall be perpetual; nor shall any alteration at any time hereafter be made in any of them; unless such alteration be agreed to in a Congress of the United States, and be afterwards confirmed by the legislatures of every State.

And Whereas it hath pleased the Great Governor of the World to incline the hearts of the legislatures we respectively represent in Congress, to approve of, and to authorize us to ratify the said Articles of Confederation and perpetual Union. Know Ye that we the undersigned delegates, by virtue of the power and authority to us given for that purpose, do by these presents, in the name and in behalf of our respective constituents, fully and entirely ratify and confirm each and every of the said Articles of Confederation and perpetual Union, and all and singular the matters and things therein contained: And we do further solemnly plight and engage the faith of our respective constituents, that they shall abide by the determinations of the United States in Congress assembled, on all questions, which by the said Confederation are submitted to them. And that the Articles thereof shall be inviolably observed by the States we respectively represent, and that the Union shall be perpetual.

In Witness whereof we have hereunto set our hands in Congress. Done at Philadelphia in the State of Pennsylvania the ninth day of July in the Year of our Lord One Thousand Seven Hundred and Seventy-Eight, and in the Third Year of the independence of America.

Agreed to by Congress 15 November 1777 In force after ratification by Maryland, 1 March 1781

And because of it nobody paid attention to it when it was in place. The individual States told the central government "fuck you" when it came to pay dues (taxes), there was no national army to speak of and States were making their own deals with foreign governments and other entities. And yes, the new Federal Government under the Articles of Confederation did print money (called a continental dollar). But it wasn't worth shit. Matter of fact if something or someone had no value it was said to "not be worth a continental!" The capper to really scare the elite was Shayes Rebellion. This one event would be a major catalyst in getting everyone back to constitutional drafting table. Daniel Shays was among the first of a long line of military veterans to get fucked over by his government. Today the Federal government lets the United States

Department of Veteran Affairs do its dirty work. Anyway, he decided that he and four thousand of his closest friends would do something about it.

Hailing from the Commonwealth of Massachusetts he and his merry band attempted to secure the United States Armory in the city of Springfield. The main argument for Shays and his followers were purely economic. Many of these men felt that the Commonwealth was asking too much in taxes and being unduly harsh in its debt collection methods. The rebellion itself was a drawn out affair lasting almost a year from summer, 1786 to summer 1787. It would take the government raising their own private militia to squash the rebellion. All in all the players knew that they would have to redo the laws of the land if it was to have any order. And this started with a stout central government. The new United States Constitution would address this. Additionally two other events would happen as a result of Shays rebellion. Not known to many, the State of Vermont was actually a Republic before it was a State. Several of the Shays Rebellion participants would seek shelter in the Republic of Vermont. Catching some of these gentlemen was at least one of the reasons Vermont gained statehood when it became the fourteenth state to join the Union. Reminders of Shays Rebellion and the reasons it started was also discussed when drafting the Eleventh Amendment to the United States Constitution. So as you can see the Rebellion was an important event into the history of America's early days.

But who was Daniel Shays? Daniel Shays was a son of Irish immigrants. During the American Revolutionary War he was active and loyal Patriot. He fought in the Battles of Bunker Hill, Lexington and

Saratoga. He resigned his commission as a result of injuries suffered in 1780. Like many other soldiers he didn't receive a fucking dime for his service. But that wasn't what pissed him off, shit he never was a wealthy man and was used to getting by on very little. What really pissed him off was the Commonwealth wanting him to pay taxes and other municipal debts knowing they hadn't paid him any money with which to make such payments. He and the others tried to take their case to the courts, but to no avail. That's when they decided to fight. Shays and the others would get their asses kicked and the ones who weren't caught scattered. As a matter of fact Shays was one of the rebels who sought refuge in the Republic of Vermont. He would eventually receive a pardon in 1788 and even be granted a pension for his military service. It was only enough to keep him and broke and allow him to die a drunk. This was a sad ending for a man that was such huge part of American history. His main nemesis was James Bowdoin, then Governor of the Commonwealth of Massachusetts. He had a very aggressive posture when it came to the Commonwealth's finances and many veterans resented him. Especially in light of the fact that the previous Governor, John Hancock was very sympathetic to delinquent tax cases. Both James Bowdoin and John Hancock would both be signatories to the United States Constitution. Governor's Bowdoin's bulldog that put down Shays Rebellion was Major General Benjamin Lincoln (and no he was not related to President of the United States Abraham Lincoln). General Lincoln showed up in western Massachusetts with ten thousand private militia, kicked what ass he had to and squashed the whole shit. General Lincoln was the most famous officer of the American Revolution many have never heard of. He was a trusted confidant of General George Washington and was highly respected in the Continental Army and amongst members of the Continental Congress. He was present at the

British Army surrenders both at Saratoga and Yorktown (where he was second in command to General George Washington). He was also present when the Continental Army surrendered after getting its ass kicked at the Battle of Charleston in 1780. Nonetheless, he would leave his mark on the American cause.

After the American Revolution, besides putting down Shays Rebellion he would serve as the United States Secretary of War, Lieutenant. Governor of the Commonwealth of Massachusetts and as the powerful head of the United States Customs House in the Port of Boston. As Secretary of War he saw firsthand how fucked up the Articles of Confederation was an instrument of law. The War Secretariat commanded an army of one hundred sixty five men and most of them weren't provisioned properly or paid at all. Shays Rebellion has such an impact on the early stages of the United States Constitution that during debate the Anti-Federalists were referred to as the "Shayites" and the Federalists were referred to as "Washingtonians." As debate got underway the word "Constitution" was even used in its description (although it is used in the Preamble). When the document was sent to the States for ratification it was referred to as the "Frame of Government." It consisted of the Preamble and seven articles. Below that were all of the signatures of the attending delegates. The Preamble reads as such:

We the People of the United States, in Order to form a more perfect Union, establish Justice, insure domestic Tranquility, provide for the common defence,[note 1] promote the general Welfare, and secure the Blessings of Liberty to ourselves and our Posterity, do ordain and establish this Constitution for the United States of America.

The Articles read as such:

Article. I.

Section. 1.

All legislative Powers herein granted shall be vested in a Congress of the United States, which shall consist of a Senate and House of Representatives.

Section. 2.

The House of Representatives shall be composed of Members chosen every second Year by the People of the several States, and the Electors in each State shall have the Qualifications requisite for Electors of the most numerous Branch of the State Legislature.

No Person shall be a Representative who shall not have attained to the Age of twenty five Years, and been seven Years a Citizen of the United States, and who shall not, when elected, be an Inhabitant of that State in which he shall be chosen.

Representatives and direct Taxes shall be apportioned among the several States which may be included within this Union, according to their respective Numbers, which shall be determined by adding to the whole Number of free Persons, including those bound to Service for a Term of Years, and excluding Indians not taxed, three fifths of all other Persons. The actual Enumeration shall be made within three Years after the first Meeting of the Congress of the United States, and within every subsequent Term of ten Years, in such Manner as they shall by Law direct. The Number of Representatives shall not exceed one for every thirty Thousand, but each State shall have at Least one Representative; and until such enumeration shall be made, the State of New Hampshire shall be entitled to chuse three, Massachusetts eight, Rhode-Island and Providence Plantations one, Connecticut five, New-York six, New Jersey four, Pennsylvania eight, Delaware one, Maryland six, Virginia ten, North Carolina five, South Carolina five, and Georgia three.

When vacancies happen in the Representation from any State, the Executive Authority thereof shall issue Writs of Election to fill such Vacancies.

The House of Representatives shall chuse their Speaker and other Officers; and shall have the sole Power of Impeachment.

Section. 3.

The Senate of the United States shall be composed of two Senators from each State, chosen by the Legislaturethereof, for six Years; and each Senator shall have one Vote.

Immediately after they shall be assembled in Consequence of the first Election, they shall be divided as equally as may be into three Classes. The Seats of the Senators of the first Class shall be vacated at the Expiration of the second Year, of the second Class at the Expiration of the fourth Year, and of the third Class at the Expiration of the sixth Year, so that one third may be chosen every second Year; and if Vacancies happen by Resignation, or otherwise, during the Recess of the Legislature of any State, the Executive thereof may make temporary Appointments until the next Meeting of the Legislature, which shall then fill such Vacancies.

No Person shall be a Senator who shall not have attained to the Age of thirty Years, and been nine Years a Citizen of the United States, and who shall not, when elected, be an Inhabitant of that State for which he shall be chosen.

The Vice President of the United States shall be President of the Senate, but shall have no Vote, unless they be equally divided.

The Senate shall chuse their other Officers, and also a President pro tempore, in the Absence of the Vice President, or when he shall exercise the Office of President of the United States.

The Senate shall have the sole Power to try all Impeachments. When sitting for that Purpose, they shall be on Oath or Affirmation. When the President of the United States is tried, the Chief Justice shall preside: And no Person shall be convicted without the Concurrence of two thirds of the Members present.

Judgment in Cases of Impeachment shall not extend further than to removal from Office, and disqualification to hold and enjoy any Office of honor, Trust or Profit under the United States: but the Party convicted shall nevertheless be liable and subject to Indictment, Trial, Judgment and Punishment, according to Law.

Section. 4.

The Times, Places and Manner of holding Elections for Senators and Representatives, shall be prescribed in each State by the Legislature thereof; but the Congress may at any time by Law make or alter such Regulations, except as to the Places of chusing Senators.

The Congress shall assemble at least once in every Year, and such Meeting shall be on the first Monday in December, unless they shall by Law appoint a different Day.

Section. 5.

Each House shall be the Judge of the Elections, Returns and Qualifications of its own Members, and a Majority of each shall constitute a Quorum to do Business; but a smaller Number may adjourn from day to day, and may be authorized to compel the Attendance of absent Members, in such Manner, and under such Penalties as each House may provide.

Each House may determine the Rules of its Proceedings, punish its Members for disorderly Behaviour, and, with the Concurrence of two thirds, expel a Member.

Each House shall keep a Journal of its Proceedings, and from time to time publish the same, excepting such Parts as may in their Judgment require Secrecy; and the Yeas and Nays of the Members of either House on any question shall, at the Desire of one fifth of those Present, be entered on the Journal.

Neither House, during the Session of Congress, shall, without the Consent of the other, adjourn for more than three days, nor to any other Place than that in which the two Houses shall be sitting.

Section. 6.

The Senators and Representatives shall receive a Compensation for their Services, to be ascertained by Law, and paid out of the Treasury of the United States. They shall in all Cases, except Treason, Felony and Breach of the Peace, be privileged from Arrest during their Attendance at the Session of their respective Houses, and in going to and returning from the same; and for any Speech or Debate in either House, they shall not be questioned in any other Place.

No Senator or Representative shall, during the Time for which he was elected, be appointed to any civil Office under the Authority of the United States, which shall have been created, or the Emoluments whereof shall have been encreased during such time; and no Person holding any Office under the United States, shall be a Member of either House during his Continuance in Office.

Section. 7.

All Bills for raising Revenue shall originate in the House of Representatives; but the Senate may propose or concur with Amendments as on other Bills.

Every Bill which shall have passed the House of Representatives and the Senate, shall, before it become a Law, be presented to the President of the United States; If he approve he shall sign it, but if not he shall return it, with his Objections to that House in which it shall have originated, who shall enter the Objections at large on their Journal, and proceed to reconsider it. If after such Reconsideration two thirds of that House shall agree to pass the Bill, it shall be sent, together with the Objections, to the other House, by which it shall likewise be reconsidered, and if approved by two thirds of that House, it shall become a Law. But in all such Cases the Votes of both Houses shall be determined by yeas and nays, and the Names of the Persons voting for and against the Bill shall be entered on the Journal of each House respectively. If any Bill shall not be returned by the President within ten Days (Sundays excepted) after it shall have been presented to him, the Same shall be a Law, in like Manner as if he had signed it, unless the Congress by their Adjournment prevent its Return, in which Case it shall not be a Law.

Every Order, Resolution, or Vote to which the Concurrence of the Senate and House of Representatives may be necessary (except on a question of Adjournment) shall be presented to the President of the United States; and before the Same shall take Effect, shall be approved by him, or being disapproved by him, shall be repassed by two thirds of the Senate and House of Representatives, according to the Rules and Limitations prescribed in the Case of a Bill.

Section. 8.

The Congress shall have Power To lay and collect Taxes, Duties, Imposts and Excises, to pay the Debts and provide for the common Defence and general Welfare of the United States; but all Duties, Imposts and Excises shall be uniform throughout the United States;

To borrow Money on the credit of the United States;

To regulate Commerce with foreign Nations, and among the several States, and with the Indian Tribes;

To establish an uniform Rule of Naturalization, and uniform Laws on the subject of Bankruptcies throughout the United States;

To coin Money, regulate the Value thereof, and of foreign Coin, and fix the Standard of Weights and Measures;

To provide for the Punishment of counterfeiting the Securities and current Coin of the United States;

To establish Post Offices and post Roads;

To promote the Progress of Science and useful Arts, by securing for limited Times to Authors and Inventors the exclusive Right to their respective Writings and Discoveries;

To constitute Tribunals inferior to the supreme Court;

To define and punish Piracies and Felonies committed on the high Seas, and Offences against the Law of Nations;

To declare War, grant Letters of Marque and Reprisal, and make Rules concerning Captures on Land and Water;

To raise and support Armies, but no Appropriation of Money to that Use shall be for a longer Term than two Years;

To provide and maintain a Navy;

To make Rules for the Government and Regulation of the land and naval Forces;

To provide for calling forth the Militia to execute the Laws of the Union, suppress Insurrections and repel Invasions;

To provide for organizing, arming, and disciplining, the Militia, and for governing such Part of them as may be employed in the Service of the United States, reserving to the States respectively, the Appointment of the Officers, and the Authority of training the Militia according to the discipline prescribed by Congress;

To exercise exclusive Legislation in all Cases whatsoever, over such District (not exceeding ten Miles square) as may, by Cession of particular States, and the Acceptance of Congress, become the Seat of the Government of the United States, and to exercise like Authority over all Places purchased by the Consent of the Legislature of the State in which the Same shall be, for the Erection of Forts, Magazines, Arsenals, dock-Yards, and other needful Buildings;—And

To make all Laws which shall be necessary and proper for carrying into Execution the foregoing Powers, and all other Powers vested by this Constitution in the Government of the United States, or in any Department or Officer thereof.

Section. 9.

The Migration or Importation of such Persons as any of the States now existing shall think proper to admit, shall not be prohibited by the Congress prior to the Year one thousand eight hundred and eight, but a Tax or duty may be imposed on such Importation, not exceeding ten dollars for each Person.

The Privilege of the Writ of Habeas Corpus shall not be suspended, unless when in Cases of Rebellion or Invasion the public Safety may require it.

No Bill of Attainder or ex post facto Law shall be passed.

No Capitation, or other direct, Tax shall be laid, unless in Proportion to the Census or enumeration herein before directed to be taken.

No Tax or Duty shall be laid on Articles exported from any State.

No Preference shall be given by any Regulation of Commerce or Revenue to the Ports of one State over those of another: nor shall Vessels bound to, or from, one State, be obliged to enter, clear, or pay Duties in another.

No Money shall be drawn from the Treasury, but in Consequence of Appropriations made by Law; and a regular Statement and Account of the Receipts and Expenditures of all public Money shall be published from time to time.

No Title of Nobility shall be granted by the United States: And no Person holding any Office of Profit or Trust under them, shall, without the Consent of the Congress, accept of any present, Emolument, Office, or Title, of any kind whatever, from any King, Prince, or foreign State.

Section. 10.

No State shall enter into any Treaty, Alliance, or Confederation; grant Letters of Marque and Reprisal; coin Money; emit Bills of Credit; make any Thing but gold and silver Coin a Tender in Payment of Debts; pass any Bill of Attainder, ex post facto Law, or Law impairing the Obligation of Contracts, or grant any Title of Nobility.

No State shall, without the Consent of the Congress, lay any Imposts or Duties on Imports or Exports, except what may be absolutely necessary for executing it's inspection Laws: and the net Produce of all Duties and Imposts, laid by any State on Imports or Exports, shall be for the Use of the Treasury of the United States; and all such Laws shall be subject to the Revision and Controul of the Congress.

No State shall, without the Consent of Congress, lay any Duty of Tonnage, keep Troops, or Ships of War in time of Peace, enter into any Agreement or Compact with another State, or with a foreign Power, or engage in War, unless actually invaded, or in such imminent Danger as will not admit of delay.

Article. II.

Section. 1.

The executive Power shall be vested in a President of the United States of America. He shall hold his Office during the Term of four Years, and, together with the Vice President, chosen for the same Term, be elected, as follows

Each State shall appoint, in such Manner as the Legislature thereof may direct, a Number of Electors, equal to the whole Number of Senators and Representatives to which the State may be entitled in the Congress: but no Senator or Representative, or Person holding an Office of Trust or Profit under the United States, shall be appointed an Elector.

The Electors shall meet in their respective States, and vote by Ballot for two Persons, of whom one at least shall not be an Inhabitant of the same State with themselves. And they shall make a List of all the Persons voted for, and of the Number of Votes for each; which List they shall sign and certify, and transmit sealed to the Seat of the Government of the United States, directed to the President of the Senate. The President of the Senate shall, in the Presence of the Senate and House of Representatives, open all the Certificates, and the Votes shall then be counted. The Person having the greatest Number of Votes shall be the President, if such Number be a Majority of the whole Number of Electors appointed; and if there be more than one who have such Majority, and have an equal Number of Votes, then the House of Representatives shall immediately chuse by Ballot one of them for President; and if no Person have a Majority, then from the five highest on the List the said House shall in like Manner chuse the President. But in chusing the President, the Votes shall be taken by States, the Representation from each State having one Vote; A quorum for this Purpose shall consist of a Member or Members from two thirds of the States, and a Majority of all the States shall be necessary to a Choice. In every Case, after the Choice of the President, the Person having the greatest Number of Votes of the Electors shall be the Vice President. But if there should remain two or more who have equal Votes, the Senate shall chuse from them by Ballot the Vice President.

The Congress may determine the Time of chusing the Electors, and the Day on which they shall give their Votes; which Day shall be the same throughout the United States.

No Person except a natural born Citizen, or a Citizen of the United States, at the time of the Adoption of this Constitution, shall be eligible to the Office of President; neither shall any Person be eligible to that Office who shall not have attained to the Age of thirty five Years, and been fourteen Years a Resident within the United States.

In Case of the Removal of the President from Office, or of his Death, Resignation, or Inability to discharge the Powers and Duties of the said Office, the Same shall devolve on the Vice President, and the Congress may by Law provide for the Case of Removal, Death, Resignation or Inability, both of the President and Vice President, declaring what Officer shall then act as President, and such Officer shall act accordingly, until the Disability be removed, or a President shall be elected.

The President shall, at stated Times, receive for his Services, a Compensation, which shall neither be encreased nor diminished during the Period for which he shall have been elected, and he shall not receive within that Period any other Emolument from the United States, or any of them.

Before he enter on the Execution of his Office, he shall take the following Oath or Affirmation:—"I do solemnly swear (or affirm) that I will faithfully execute the Office of President of the United States, and will to the best of my Ability, preserve, protect and defend the Constitution of the United States."

Section. 2.

The President shall be Commander in Chief of the Army and Navy of the United States, and of the Militia of the several States, when called into the actual Service of the United States; he may require the Opinion, in writing, of the principal Officer in each of the executive Departments, upon any Subject relating to the Duties of their respective Offices, and he shall have Power to grant Reprieves and Pardons for Offences against the United States, except in Cases of Impeachment.

He shall have Power, by and with the Advice and Consent of the Senate, to make Treaties, provided two thirds of the Senators present concur; and he shall nominate, and by and with the Advice and Consent of the Senate, shall appoint Ambassadors, other public Ministers and Consuls, Judges of the supreme Court, and all other Officers of the United States, whose Appointments are not herein otherwise provided for, and which shall be established by Law: but the Congress may by Law vest the Appointment of such inferior Officers, as they think proper, in the President alone, in the Courts of Law, or in the Heads of Departments.

The President shall have Power to fill up all Vacancies that may happen during the Recess of the Senate, by granting Commissions which shall expire at the End of their next Session.

Section. 3.

He shall from time to time give to the Congress Information of the State of the Union, and recommend to their Consideration such Measures as he shall judge necessary and expedient; he may, on extraordinary Occasions, convene both Houses, or either of them, and in Case of Disagreement between them, with Respect to the Time of Adjournment, he may adjourn them to such Time as he shall think proper; he shall receive Ambassadors and other public Ministers; he shall take Care that the Laws be faithfully executed, and shall Commission all the Officers of the United States.

Section. 4.

The President, Vice President and all civil Officers of the United States, shall be removed from Office on Impeachment for, and Conviction of, Treason, Bribery, or other high Crimes and Misdemeanors.

Article III.

Section. 1.

The judicial Power of the United States, shall be vested in one supreme Court, and in such inferior Courts as the Congress may from time to time ordain and establish. The Judges, both of the supreme and inferior Courts, shall hold their Offices during good Behaviour, and shall, at stated Times, receive for their Services, a Compensation, which shall not be diminished during their Continuance in Office.

Section. 2.

The judicial Power shall extend to all Cases, in Law and Equity, arising under this Constitution, the Laws of the United States, and Treaties made, or which shall be made, under their Authority;—to all Cases affecting Ambassadors, other public Ministers and Consuls;—to all Cases of admiralty and maritime Jurisdiction;—to Controversies to which the United States shall be a Party;—to Controversies between two or more States;— between a State and Citizens of another State,— between Citizens of different States,—between Citizens of the same State claiming Lands under Grants of different States, and between a State, or the Citizens thereof, and foreign States, Citizens or Subjects.

In all Cases affecting Ambassadors, other public Ministers and Consuls, and those in which a State shall be Party, the supreme Court shall have original Jurisdiction. In all the other Cases before mentioned, the supreme Court shall have appellate Jurisdiction, both as to Law and Fact, with such Exceptions, and under such Regulations as the Congress shall make.

The Trial of all Crimes, except in Cases of Impeachment, shall be by Jury; and such Trial shall be held in the State where the said Crimes shall have been committed; but when not committed within any State, the Trial shall be at such Place or Places as the Congress may by Law have directed.

Section. 3.

Treason against the United States, shall consist only in levying War against them, or in adhering to their Enemies, giving them Aid and Comfort. No Person shall be convicted of Treason unless on the Testimony of two Witnesses to the same overt Act, or on Confession in open Court.

The Congress shall have Power to declare the Punishment of Treason, but no Attainder of Treason shall work Corruption of Blood, or Forfeiture except during the Life of the Person attainted.

Article. IV.

Section. 1.

Full Faith and Credit shall be given in each State to the public Acts, Records, and judicial Proceedings of every other State. And the Congress may by general Laws prescribe the Manner in which such Acts, Records and Proceedings shall be proved, and the Effect thereof.

Section. 2.
The Citizens of each State shall be entitled to all Privileges and Immunities of Citizens in the several States.

A Person charged in any State with Treason, Felony, or other Crime, who shall flee from Justice, and be found in another State, shall on Demand of the executive Authority of the State from which he fled, be delivered up, to be removed to the State having Jurisdiction of the Crime.

No Person held to Service or Labour in one State, under the Laws thereof, escaping into another, shall, in Consequence of any Law or Regulation therein, be discharged from such Service or Labour, but shall be delivered up on Claim of the Party to whom such Service or Labour may be due.

Section. 3.
New States may be admitted by the Congress into this Union; but no new State shall be formed or erected within the Jurisdiction of any other State; nor any State be formed by the Junction of two or more States, or Parts of States, without the Consent of the Legislatures of the States concerned as well as of the Congress.

The Congress shall have Power to dispose of and make all needful Rules and Regulations respecting the Territory or other Property belonging to the United States; and nothing in this Constitution shall be so construed as to Prejudice any Claims of the United States, or of any particular State.

Section. 4.

The United States shall guarantee to every State in this Union a Republican Form of Government, and shall protect each of them against Invasion; and on Application of the Legislature, or of the Executive (when the Legislature cannot be convened), against domestic Violence.

Article. V.

The Congress, whenever two thirds of both Houses shall deem it necessary, shall propose Amendments to this Constitution, or, on the Application of the Legislatures of two thirds of the several States, shall call a Convention for proposing Amendments, which, in either Case, shall be valid to all Intents and Purposes, as Part of this Constitution, when ratified by the Legislatures of three fourths of the several States, or by Conventions in three fourths thereof, as the one or the other Mode of Ratification may be proposed by the Congress; Provided that no Amendment which may be made prior to the Year One thousand eight hundred and eight shall in any Manner affect the first and fourth Clauses in the Ninth Section of the first Article; and that no State, without its Consent, shall be deprived of its equal Suffrage in the Senate.

Article. VI.

All Debts contracted and Engagements entered into, before the Adoption of this Constitution, shall be as valid against the United States under this Constitution, as under the Confederation.

This Constitution, and the Laws of the United States which shall be made in Pursuance thereof; and all Treaties made, or which shall be made, under the Authority of the United States, shall be the supreme Law of the Land; and the Judges in every State shall be bound thereby, any Thing in the Constitution or Laws of any State to the Contrary notwithstanding.

The Senators and Representatives before mentioned, and the Members of the several State Legislatures, and all executive and judicial Officers, both of the United States and of the several States, shall be bound by Oath or Affirmation, to support this Constitution; but no religious Test shall ever be required as a Qualification to any Office or public Trust under the United States.

Article. VII.

The Ratification of the Conventions of nine States, shall be sufficient for the Establishment of this Constitution between the States so ratifying the Same.

The Word, "the," being interlined between the seventh and eighth Lines of the first Page, The Word "Thirty" being partly written on an Erazure in the fifteenth Line of the first Page, The Words "is tried" being interlined between the thirty second and thirty third Lines of the first Page and the Word "the" being interlined between the forty third and forty fourth Lines of the second Page.

You can read it not read it, it's up to you. However the key to the United States Constitution is the Section Eight of Article One. This Section is all about money and what the Federal Government can do with the money once it gets it. Now, yes, there is other shit in there too. Notable the Federal Government can build an army, navy and post office. Also the Government gets to determine who is a citizen through the power of defining the procedure for Naturalization per Section Eight. So you can think of it as the military protect the money, the post office is set up so you can just send the money in (basically we're too lazy to come it) and they get to say what people get to enjoy all the new shit we gonna build when we let you become a citizen. However, the document is not perfect and while it has stood the test of time there are those that argue some change is still due. From this authors perspective the "Three-Fifths Compromise," should be done away with. Yes the Fourteenth and Fifteenth Amendments nullify the text but why not just get rid of it? It's a stain on the document. Another item that should get flushed is the Electoral College. The system is flawed if a Presidential Candidate can lose the popular vote and still get elected by winning the Electoral vote. It's bullshit. Or, as the Italians say, "che a una stronzata!"

The other document that is worth noting is the Universal Declaration of Human Rights.

The text reads as such:

PREAMBLE

Whereas recognition of the inherent dignity and of the equal and inalienable rights of all members of the human family is the foundation of freedom, justice and peace in the world,

Whereas disregard and contempt for human rights have resulted in barbarous acts which have outraged the conscience of mankind, and the advent of a world in which human beings shall enjoy freedom of speech and belief and freedom from fear and want has been proclaimed as the highest aspiration of the common people,

Whereas it is essential, if man is not to be compelled to have recourse, as a last resort, to rebellion against tyranny and oppression, that human rights should be protected by the rule of law,

Whereas it is essential to promote the development of friendly relations between nations,

Whereas the peoples of the United Nations have in the Charter reaffirmed their faith in fundamental human rights, in the dignity and worth of the human person and in the equal rights of men and women and have determined to promote social progress and better standards of life in larger freedom,

Whereas Member States have pledged themselves to achieve, in cooperation with the United Nations, the promotion of universal respect for and observance of human rights and fundamental freedoms,

Whereas a common understanding of these rights and freedoms is of the greatest importance for the full realization of this pledge,

Now, Therefore THE GENERAL ASSEMBLY proclaims THIS UNIVERSAL DECLARATION OF HUMAN RIGHTS as a common standard of achievement for all peoples and all nations, to the end that every individual and every organ of society, keeping this Declaration constantly in mind, shall strive by teaching and education to promote respect for these rights and freedoms and by progressive measures, national and international, to secure their universal and effective recognition and observance, both among the peoples of Member States themselves and among the peoples of territories under their jurisdiction.

Article 1.

- All human beings are born free and equal in dignity and rights. They are endowed with reason and conscience and should act towards one another in a spirit of brotherhood.

Article 2.

- Everyone is entitled to all the rights and freedoms set forth in this Declaration, without distinction of any kind, such as race, colour, sex, language, religion, political or other opinion, national or social origin, property, birth or other status. Furthermore, no distinction shall be made on the basis of the political, jurisdictional or international status of the country or territory to which a person belongs, whether it be independent, trust, non-self-governing or under any other limitation of sovereignty.

Article 3.

- Everyone has the right to life, liberty and security of person.

Article 4.

- No one shall be held in slavery or servitude; slavery and the slave trade shall be prohibited in all their forms.

Article 5.

- No one shall be subjected to torture or to cruel, inhuman or degrading treatment or punishment.

Article 6.

- Everyone has the right to recognition everywhere as a person before the law.

Article 7.

- All are equal before the law and are entitled without any discrimination to equal protection of the law. All are entitled to equal protection against any discrimination in violation of this Declaration and against any incitement to such discrimination.

Article 8.

- Everyone has the right to an effective remedy by the competent national tribunals for acts violating the fundamental rights granted him by the constitution or by law.

Article 9.

- No one shall be subjected to arbitrary arrest, detention or exile.

Article 10.

- Everyone is entitled in full equality to a fair and public hearing by an independent and impartial tribunal, in the determination of his rights and obligations and of any criminal charge against him.

Article 11.

- (1) Everyone charged with a penal offence has the right to be presumed innocent until proved guilty according to law in a public trial at which he has had all the guarantees necessary for his defence.
- (2) No one shall be held guilty of any penal offence on account of any act or omission which did not constitute a penal offence, under national or international law, at the time when it was committed. Nor shall a heavier penalty be imposed than the one that was applicable at the time the penal offence was committed.

Article 12.

- No one shall be subjected to arbitrary interference with his privacy, family, home or correspondence, nor to attacks upon his honour and reputation. Everyone has the right to the protection of the law against such interference or attacks.

Article 13.

- (1) Everyone has the right to freedom of movement and residence within the borders of each state.
- (2) Everyone has the right to leave any country, including his own, and to return to his country.

Article 14.

- (1) Everyone has the right to seek and to enjoy in other countries asylum from persecution.
- (2) This right may not be invoked in the case of prosecutions genuinely arising from non-political crimes or from acts contrary to the purposes and principles of the United Nations.

Article 15.

- (1) Everyone has the right to a nationality.
- (2) No one shall be arbitrarily deprived of his nationality nor denied the right to change his nationality.

Article 16.

- (1) Men and women of full age, without any limitation due to race, nationality or religion, have the right to marry and to found a family. They are entitled to equal rights as to marriage, during marriage and at its dissolution.

- (2) Marriage shall be entered into only with the free and full consent of the intending spouses.
- (3) The family is the natural and fundamental group unit of society and is entitled to protection by society and the State.

Article 17.

- (1) Everyone has the right to own property alone as well as in association with others.
- (2) No one shall be arbitrarily deprived of his property.

Article 18.

- Everyone has the right to freedom of thought, conscience and religion; this right includes freedom to change his religion or belief, and freedom, either alone or in community with others and in public or private, to manifest his religion or belief in teaching, practice, worship and observance.
-

Article 19.

- Everyone has the right to freedom of opinion and expression; this right includes freedom to hold opinions without interference and to seek, receive and impart information and ideas through any media and regardless of frontiers.

Article 20.

- (1) Everyone has the right to freedom of peaceful assembly and association.
- (2) No one may be compelled to belong to an association.

Article 21.

- (1) Everyone has the right to take part in the government of his country, directly or through freely chosen representatives.
- (2) Everyone has the right of equal access to public service in his country.
- (3) The will of the people shall be the basis of the authority of government; this will shall be expressed in periodic and genuine elections which shall be by universal and equal suffrage and shall be held by secret vote or by equivalent free voting procedures.

Article 22.

- Everyone, as a member of society, has the right to social security and is entitled to realization, through national effort and international co-operation and in accordance with the organization and resources of each State, of the economic, social and cultural rights indispensable for his dignity and the free development of his personality.

Article 23.

- (1) Everyone has the right to work, to free choice of employment, to just and favourable conditions of work and to protection against unemployment.
- (2) Everyone, without any discrimination, has the right to equal pay for equal work.
- (3) Everyone who works has the right to just and favourable remuneration ensuring for himself and his family an existence worthy of human dignity, and supplemented, if necessary, by other means of social protection.
- (4) Everyone has the right to form and to join trade unions for the protection of his interests.

Article 24.

- Everyone has the right to rest and leisure, including reasonable limitation of working hours and periodic holidays with pay.

Article 25.

- (1) Everyone has the right to a standard of living adequate for the health and well-being of himself and of his family, including food, clothing, housing and medical care and necessary social services, and the right to security in the event of unemployment, sickness, disability, widowhood, old age or other lack of livelihood in circumstances beyond his control.

- (2) Motherhood and childhood are entitled to special care and assistance. All children, whether born in or out of wedlock, shall enjoy the same social protection.

Article 26.

- (1) Everyone has the right to education. Education shall be free, at least in the elementary and fundamental stages. Elementary education shall be compulsory. Technical and professional education shall be made generally available and higher education shall be equally accessible to all on the basis of merit.
- (2) Education shall be directed to the full development of the human personality and to the strengthening of respect for human rights and fundamental freedoms. It shall promote understanding, tolerance and friendship among all nations, racial or religious groups, and shall further the activities of the United Nations for the maintenance of peace.
- (3) Parents have a prior right to choose the kind of education that shall be given to their children.

Article 27.

- (1) Everyone has the right freely to participate in the cultural life of the community, to enjoy the arts and to share in scientific advancement and its benefits.
- (2) Everyone has the right to the protection of the moral and material interests resulting from any scientific, literary or artistic production of which he is the author.

Article 28.

- Everyone is entitled to a social and international order in which the rights and freedoms set forth in this Declaration can be fully realized.

Article 29.

- (1) Everyone has duties to the community in which alone the free and full development of his personality is possible.
- (2) In the exercise of his rights and freedoms, everyone shall be subject only to such limitations as are determined by law solely for the purpose of securing due recognition and respect for the rights and freedoms of others and of meeting the just requirements of morality, public order and the general welfare in a democratic society.
- (3) These rights and freedoms may in no case be exercised contrary to the purposes and principles of the United Nations.

Article 30.

- Nothing in this Declaration may be interpreted as implying for any State, group or person any right to engage in any activity or to perform any act aimed at the destruction of any of the rights and freedoms set forth herein.

As World War Two was raging and knowledge of how brutal the fucking Nazis were became a known reality the Allies decided that there were four main war goals. Known as the Four Freedoms they were:

Freedom of speech

Freedom of religion

Freedom from fear

Freedom from want

It is from these goals that the Universal Declaration of Human Rights was established. Its passage is the only known document to detail certain rights that ALL human beings are entitled to just for sucking up oxygen on the planet. It's damn good too. Problem is very few governments around the world actually follow these rights. Not surprising since the United Nations is a fairy tale organization when its member nations don't give a fuck about an idea, which is often. Even the Declaration's signatories violate its rights.

Its signers include the following nations:

- Afghanistan
- Argentina
- Australia
- Belgium
- Bolivia
- Brazil
- Burma
- Canada
- Chile
- China
- Colombia
- Costa Rica
- Cuba

- Denmark
- Dominican Republic
- Ecuador
- Egypt
- El Salvador
- Ethiopia
- France
- Greece
- Guatemala
- Haiti
- Iceland
- India
- Iran
- Iraq
- Lebanon
- Liberia
- Luxembourg
- Mexico
- Netherlands
- New Zealand
- Nicaragua
- Norway
- Pakistan
- Panama
- Paraguay
- Peru
- Philippines
- Siam
- Sweden

- Syria
- Turkey
- United Kingdom
- United States
- Uruguay
- Venezuela

The last document relevant to the discussion is the Magna Carta.

Its text (as translated) reads as such:

JOHN, by the grace of God King of England, Lord of Ireland, Duke of Normandy and Aquitaine, and Count of Anjou, to his arch-bishops, bishops, abbots, earls, barons, justices, foresters, sheriffs, stewards, servants, and to all his officials and loyal subjects, Greeting.

KNOW THAT BEFORE GOD, for the health of our soul and those of our ancestors and heirs, to the honour of God, the exaltation of the holy Church, and the better ordering of our kingdom, at the advice of our reverend fathers Stephen, archbishop of Canterbury, primate of all England, and cardinal of the holy Roman Church, Henry archbishop of Dublin, William bishop of London, Peter bishop of Winchester, Jocelin bishop of Bath and Glastonbury, Hugh bishop of Lincoln, Walter bishop of Worcester, William bishop of Coventry, Benedict bishop of Rochester, Master Pandulf subdeacon and member of the papal household, Brother Aymeric master of the knighthood of the Temple in England, William Marshal earl of Pembroke, William earl of Salisbury, William earl of Warren, William earl of Arundel, Alan of Galloway constable of Scotland, Warin fitz Gerald, Peter fitz Herbert, Hubert de Burgh seneschal of Poitou, Hugh de Neville, Matthew fitz Herbert, Thomas Basset, Alan Basset, Philip Daubeny, Robert de Roppeley, John Marshal, John fitz Hugh, and other loyal subjects:

✠ (1) FIRST, THAT WE HAVE GRANTED TO GOD, and by this present charter have confirmed for us and our heirs in perpetuity, that the English Church shall be free, and shall have its rights undiminished, and its liberties unimpaired. That we wish this so to be observed, appears from the fact that of our own free will, before the outbreak of the present dispute between us and our barons, we granted and confirmed by charter the freedom of the Church's elections - a right reckoned to be of the greatest necessity and importance to it - and caused this to be confirmed by Pope Innocent III. This freedom we shall observe ourselves, and desire to be observed in good faith by our heirs in perpetuity.

TO ALL FREE MEN OF OUR KINGDOM we have also granted, for us and our heirs for ever, all the liberties written out below, to have and to keep for them and their heirs, of us and our heirs:

(2) If any earl, baron, or other person that holds lands directly of the Crown, for military service, shall die, and at his death his heir shall be of full age and owe a 'relief', the heir shall have his inheritance on payment of the ancient scale of 'relief'. That is to say, the heir or heirs of an earl shall pay £100 for the entire earl's barony, the heir or heirs of a knight 100s. at most for the entire knight's 'fee', and any man that owes less shall pay less, in accordance with the ancient usage of 'fees'.

(3) But if the heir of such a person is under age and a ward, when he comes of age he shall have his inheritance without 'relief' or fine.

(4) The guardian of the land of an heir who is under age shall take from it only reasonable revenues, customary dues, and feudal services. He shall do this without destruction or damage to men or property. If we have given the guardianship of the land to a sheriff, or to any person answerable to us for the revenues, and he commits destruction or damage, we will exact compensation from him, and the land shall be entrusted to two worthy and prudent men of the same 'fee', who shall be answerable to us for the revenues, or to the person to whom we have assigned them. If we have given or sold to anyone the guardianship of such land, and he causes destruction or damage, he shall lose the guardianship of it, and it shall be handed over to two worthy and prudent men of the same 'fee', who shall be similarly answerable to us.

(5) For so long as a guardian has guardianship of such land, he shall maintain the houses, parks, fish preserves, ponds, mills, and everything else pertaining to it, from the revenues of the land itself. When the heir comes of age, he shall restore the whole land to him, stocked with plough teams and such implements of husbandry as the season demands and the revenues from the land can reasonably bear.

(6) Heirs may be given in marriage, but not to someone of lower social standing. Before a marriage takes place, it shall be made known to the heir's next-of-kin.

(7) At her husband's death, a widow may have her marriage portion and inheritance at once and without trouble. She shall pay nothing

for her dower, marriage portion, or any inheritance that she and her husband held jointly on the day of his death. She may remain in her husband's house for forty days after his death, and within this period her dower shall be assigned to her.

(8) No widow shall be compelled to marry, so long as she wishes to remain without a husband. But she must give security that she will not marry without royal consent, if she holds her lands of the Crown, or without the consent of whatever other lord she may hold them of.

(9) Neither we nor our officials will seize any land or rent in payment of a debt, so long as the debtor has movable goods sufficient to discharge the debt. A debtor's sureties shall not be distrained upon so long as the debtor himself can discharge his debt. If, for lack of means, the debtor is unable to discharge his debt, his sureties shall be answerable for it. If they so desire, they may have the debtor's lands and rents until they have received satisfaction for the debt that they paid for him, unless the debtor can show that he has settled his obligations to them.

* (10) If anyone who has borrowed a sum of money from Jews dies before the debt has been repaid, his heir shall pay no interest on the debt for so long as he remains under age, irrespective of whom he holds his lands. If such a debt falls into the hands of the Crown, it will take nothing except the principal sum specified in the bond.

* (11) If a man dies owing money to Jews, his wife may have her dower and pay nothing towards the debt from it. If he leaves children that are under age, their needs may also be provided for on a scale

appropriate to the size of his holding of lands. The debt is to be paid out of the residue, reserving the service due to his feudal lords. Debts owed to persons other than Jews are to be dealt with similarly.

* (12) No 'scutage' or 'aid' may be levied in our kingdom without its general consent, unless it is for the ransom of our person, to make our eldest son a knight, and (once) to marry our eldest daughter. For these purposes only a reasonable 'aid' may be levied. 'Aids' from the city of London are to be treated similarly.

+ (13) The city of London shall enjoy all its ancient liberties and free customs, both by land and by water. We also will and grant that all other cities, boroughs, towns, and ports shall enjoy all their liberties and free customs.

* (14) To obtain the general consent of the realm for the assessment of an 'aid' - except in the three cases specified above - or a 'scutage', we will cause the archbishops, bishops, abbots, earls, and greater barons to be summoned individually by letter. To those who hold lands directly of us we will cause a general summons to be issued, through the sheriffs and other officials, to come together on a fixed day (of which at least forty days notice shall be given) and at a fixed place. In all letters of summons, the cause of the summons will be stated. When a summons has been issued, the business appointed for the day shall go forward in accordance with the resolution of those present, even if not all those who were summoned have appeared.

* (15) In future we will allow no one to levy an 'aid' from his free men, except to ransom his person, to make his eldest son a knight, and

(once) to marry his eldest daughter. For these purposes only a reasonable 'aid' may be levied.

(16) No man shall be forced to perform more service for a knight's 'fee', or other free holding of land, than is due from it.

(17) Ordinary lawsuits shall not follow the royal court around, but shall be held in a fixed place.

(18) Inquests of novel disseisin, mort d'ancestor, and darrein presentment shall be taken only in their proper county court. We ourselves, or in our absence abroad our chief justice, will send two justices to each county four times a year, and these justices, with four knights of the county elected by the county itself, shall hold the assizes in the county court, on the day and in the place where the court meets.

(19) If any assizes cannot be taken on the day of the county court, as many knights and freeholders shall afterwards remain behind, of those who have attended the court, as will suffice for the administration of justice, having regard to the volume of business to be done.

(20) For a trivial offence, a free man shall be fined only in proportion to the degree of his offence, and for a serious offence correspondingly, but not so heavily as to deprive him of his livelihood. In the same way, a merchant shall be spared his merchandise, and a villein the implements of his husbandry, if they fall upon the mercy of a royal court. None of these fines shall be imposed except by the assessment on oath of reputable men of the neighbourhood.

(21) Earls and barons shall be fined only by their equals, and in proportion to the gravity of their offence.

(22) A fine imposed upon the lay property of a clerk in holy orders shall be assessed upon the same principles, without reference to the value of his ecclesiastical benefice.

(23) No town or person shall be forced to build bridges over rivers except those with an ancient obligation to do so.

(24) No sheriff, constable, coroners, or other royal officials are to hold lawsuits that should be held by the royal justices.

* (25) Every county, hundred, wapentake, and tithing shall remain at its ancient rent, without increase, except the royal demesne manors.

(26) If at the death of a man who holds a lay 'fee' of the Crown, a sheriff or royal official produces royal letters patent of summons for a debt due to the Crown, it shall be lawful for them to seize and list movable goods found in the lay 'fee' of the dead man to the value of the debt, as assessed by worthy men. Nothing shall be removed until the whole debt is paid, when the residue shall be given over to the executors to carry out the dead man's will. If no debt is due to the Crown, all the movable goods shall be regarded as the property of the dead man, except the reasonable shares of his wife and children.

* (27) If a free man dies intestate, his movable goods are to be distributed by his next-of-kin and friends, under the supervision of the Church. The rights of his debtors are to be preserved.

(28) No constable or other royal official shall take corn or other movable goods from any man without immediate payment, unless the seller voluntarily offers postponement of this.

(29) No constable may compel a knight to pay money for castle-guard if the knight is willing to undertake the guard in person, or with reasonable excuse to supply some other fit man to do it. A knight taken or sent on military service shall be excused from castle-guard for the period of this service.

(30) No sheriff, royal official, or other person shall take horses or carts for transport from any free man, without his consent.

(31) Neither we nor any royal official will take wood for our castle, or for any other purpose, without the consent of the owner.

(32) We will not keep the lands of people convicted of felony in our hand for longer than a year and a day, after which they shall be returned to the lords of the 'fees' concerned.

(33) All fish-weirs shall be removed from the Thames, the Medway, and throughout the whole of England, except on the sea coast.

(34) The writ called precipe shall not in future be issued to anyone in respect of any holding of land, if a free man could thereby be deprived of the right of trial in his own lord's court.

(35) There shall be standard measures of wine, ale, and corn (the London quarter), throughout the kingdom. There shall also be a standard

width of dyed cloth, russet, and haberject, namely two ells within the selvedges. Weights are to be standardised similarly.

(36) In future nothing shall be paid or accepted for the issue of a writ of inquisition of life or limbs. It shall be given gratis, and not refused.

(37) If a man holds land of the Crown by 'fee-farm', 'socage', or 'burgage', and also holds land of someone else for knight's service, we will not have guardianship of his heir, nor of the land that belongs to the other person's 'fee', by virtue of the 'fee-farm', 'socage', or 'burgage', unless the 'fee-farm' owes knight's service. We will not have the guardianship of a man's heir, or of land that he holds of someone else, by reason of any small property that he may hold of the Crown for a service of knives, arrows, or the like.

(38) In future no official shall place a man on trial upon his own unsupported statement, without producing credible witnesses to the truth of it.

+ (39) No free man shall be seized or imprisoned, or stripped of his rights or possessions, or outlawed or exiled, or deprived of his standing in any way, nor will we proceed with force against him, or send others to do so, except by the lawful judgment of his equals or by the law of the land.

+ (40) To no one will we sell, to no one deny or delay right or justice.

(41) All merchants may enter or leave England unharmed and without fear, and may stay or travel within it, by land or water, for purposes of trade, free from all illegal exactions, in accordance with ancient and

lawful customs. This, however, does not apply in time of war to merchants from a country that is at war with us. Any such merchants found in our country at the outbreak of war shall be detained without injury to their persons or property, until we or our chief justice have discovered how our own merchants are being treated in the country at war with us. If our own merchants are safe they shall be safe too.

* (42) In future it shall be lawful for any man to leave and return to our kingdom unharmed and without fear, by land or water, preserving his allegiance to us, except in time of war, for some short period, for the common benefit of the realm. People that have been imprisoned or outlawed in accordance with the law of the land, people from a country that is at war with us, and merchants - who shall be dealt with as stated above - are excepted from this provision.

(43) If a man holds lands of any 'escheat' such as the 'honour' of Wallingford, Nottingham, Boulogne, Lancaster, or of other 'escheats' in our hand that are baronies, at his death his heir shall give us only the 'relief' and service that he would have made to the baron, had the barony been in the baron's hand. We will hold the 'escheat' in the same manner as the baron held it.

(44) People who live outside the forest need not in future appear before the royal justices of the forest in answer to general summonses, unless they are actually involved in proceedings or are sureties for someone who has been seized for a forest offence.

* (45) We will appoint as justices, constables, sheriffs, or other officials, only men that know the law of the realm and are minded to keep it well.

(46) All barons who have founded abbeys, and have charters of English kings or ancient tenure as evidence of this, may have guardianship of them when there is no abbot, as is their due.

(47) All forests that have been created in our reign shall at once be disafforested. River-banks that have been enclosed in our reign shall be treated similarly.

*(48) All evil customs relating to forests and warrens, foresters, warreners, sheriffs and their servants, or river-banks and their wardens, are at once to be investigated in every county by twelve sworn knights of the county, and within forty days of their enquiry the evil customs are to be abolished completely and irrevocably. But we, or our chief justice if we are not in England, are first to be informed.

* (49) We will at once return all hostages and charters delivered up to us by Englishmen as security for peace or for loyal service.

* (50) We will remove completely from their offices the kinsmen of Gerard de Athée, and in future they shall hold no offices in England. The people in question are Engelard de Cigogné, Peter, Guy, and Andrew de Chanceaux, Guy de Cigogné, Geoffrey de Martigny and his brothers, Philip Marc and his brothers, with Geoffrey his nephew, and all their followers.

* (51) As soon as peace is restored, we will remove from the kingdom all the foreign knights, bowmen, their attendants, and the mercenaries that have come to it, to its harm, with horses and arms.

* (52) To any man whom we have deprived or dispossessed of lands, castles, liberties, or rights, without the lawful judgment of his equals, we will at once restore these. In cases of dispute the matter shall be resolved by the judgment of the twenty-five barons referred to below in the clause for securing the peace (§61). In cases, however, where a man was deprived or dispossessed of something without the lawful judgment of his equals by our father King Henry or our brother King Richard, and it remains in our hands or is held by others under our warranty, we shall have respite for the period commonly allowed to Crusaders, unless a law-suit had been begun, or an enquiry had been made at our order, before we took the Cross as a Crusader. On our return from the Crusade, or if we abandon it, we will at once render justice in full.

* (53) We shall have similar respite in rendering justice in connexion with forests that are to be disafforested, or to remain forests, when these were first afforested by our father Henry or our brother Richard; with the guardianship of lands in another person's 'fee', when we have hitherto had this by virtue of a 'fee' held of us for knight's service by a third party; and with abbeys founded in another person's 'fee', in which the lord of the 'fee' claims to own a right. On our return from the Crusade, or if we abandon it, we will at once do full justice to complaints about these matters.

(54) No one shall be arrested or imprisoned on the appeal of a woman for the death of any person except her husband.

* (55) All fines that have been given to us unjustly and against the law of the land, and all fines that we have exacted unjustly, shall be entirely remitted or the matter decided by a majority judgment of the twenty-five barons referred to below in the clause for securing the peace (§61)

together with Stephen, archbishop of Canterbury, if he can be present, and such others as he wishes to bring with him. If the archbishop cannot be present, proceedings shall continue without him, provided that if any of the twenty-five barons has been involved in a similar suit himself, his judgment shall be set aside, and someone else chosen and sworn in his place, as a substitute for the single occasion, by the rest of the twenty-five.

(56) If we have deprived or dispossessed any Welshmen of land, liberties, or anything else in England or in Wales, without the lawful judgment of their equals, these are at once to be returned to them. A dispute on this point shall be determined in the Marches by the judgment of equals. English law shall apply to holdings of land in England, Welsh law to those in Wales, and the law of the Marches to those in the Marches. The Welsh shall treat us and ours in the same way.

* (57) In cases where a Welshman was deprived or dispossessed of anything, without the lawful judgment of his equals, by our father King Henry or our brother King Richard, and it remains in our hands or is held by others under our warranty, we shall have respite for the period commonly allowed to Crusaders, unless a lawsuit had been begun, or an enquiry had been made at our order, before we took the Cross as a Crusader. But on our return from the Crusade, or if we abandon it, we will at once do full justice according to the laws of Wales and the said regions.

* (58) We will at once return the son of Llywelyn, all Welsh hostages, and the charters delivered to us as security for the peace.

* (59) With regard to the return of the sisters and hostages of Alexander, king of Scotland, his liberties and his rights, we will treat

him in the same way as our other barons of England, unless it appears from the charters that we hold from his father William, formerly king of Scotland, that he should be treated otherwise. This matter shall be resolved by the judgment of his equals in our court.

(60) All these customs and liberties that we have granted shall be observed in our kingdom in so far as concerns our own relations with our subjects. Let all men of our kingdom, whether clergy or laymen, observe them similarly in their relations with their own men.

* (61) SINCE WE HAVE GRANTED ALL THESE THINGS for God, for the better ordering of our kingdom, and to allay the discord that has arisen between us and our barons, and since we desire that they shall be enjoyed in their entirety, with lasting strength, for ever, we give and grant to the barons the following security:

The barons shall elect twenty-five of their number to keep, and cause to be observed with all their might, the peace and liberties granted and confirmed to them by this charter.

If we, our chief justice, our officials, or any of our servants offend in any respect against any man, or transgress any of the articles of the peace or of this security, and the offence is made known to four of the said twenty-five barons, they shall come to us - or in our absence from the kingdom to the chief justice - to declare it and claim immediate redress. If we, or in our absence abroad the chief justice, make no redress within forty days, reckoning from the day on which the offence was declared to us or to him, the four barons shall refer the matter to the rest of the twenty-five barons, who may distrain upon and assail us in every way possible, with the support of the whole community of the land, by seizing our castles, lands, possessions, or anything else saving only our own person and those of the queen and our children, until they have secured such redress as they have determined upon. Having secured the redress, they may then resume their normal obedience to us.

Any man who so desires may take an oath to obey the commands of the twenty-five barons for the achievement of these ends, and to join with them in assailing us to the utmost of his power. We give public and free permission to take this oath to any man who so desires, and at no time will we prohibit any man from taking it. Indeed, we will compel any of our subjects who are unwilling to take it to swear it at our command.

If one of the twenty-five barons dies or leaves the country, or is prevented in any other way from discharging his duties, the rest of them shall choose another baron in his place, at their discretion, who shall be duly sworn in as they were.

In the event of disagreement among the twenty-five barons on any matter referred to them for decision, the verdict of the majority present shall have the same validity as a unanimous verdict of the whole twenty-five, whether these were all present or some of those summoned were unwilling or unable to appear.

The twenty-five barons shall swear to obey all the above articles faithfully, and shall cause them to be obeyed by others to the best of their power.

We will not seek to procure from anyone, either by our own efforts or those of a third party, anything by which any part of these concessions or liberties might be revoked or diminished. Should such a thing be procured, it shall be null and void and we will at no time make use of it, either ourselves or through a third party.

* (62) We have remitted and pardoned fully to all men any ill-will, hurt, or grudges that have arisen between us and our subjects, whether clergy or laymen, since the beginning of the dispute. We have in addition remitted fully, and for our own part have also pardoned, to all clergy and laymen any offences committed as a result of the said dispute between Easter in the sixteenth year of our reign (i.e. 1215) and the restoration of peace.

In addition we have caused letters patent to be made for the barons, bearing witness to this security and to the concessions set out above, over the seals of Stephen archbishop of Canterbury, Henry archbishop of Dublin, the other bishops named above, and Master Pandulf.

* (63) IT IS ACCORDINGLY OUR WISH AND COMMAND that the English Church shall be free, and that men in our kingdom shall have and keep all these liberties, rights, and concessions, well and peaceably in their fullness and entirety for them and their heirs, of us and our heirs, in all things and all places for ever.

Both we and the barons have sworn that all this shall be observed in good faith and without deceit. Witness the abovementioned people and many others.

Given by our hand in the meadow that is called Runnymede, between Windsor and Staines, on the fifteenth day of June in the seventeenth year of our reign (i.e. 1215: the new regnal year began on 28 May).

The Magna Carta is a nine hundred year old document that laid the foundation for many "rights" conversations. It was primarily laid out to get rich land owners off the then English King John's back. In the Anglo Saxon world it is one of the earliest edicts that addressed citizen rights. In addition to its influence on the original United States Constitution it remnants can be clearly seen in the Articles of Confederation and the Universal Declaration of Human Rights.

Chapter 15

❧

Summary

As we look at the United States Constitution as a whole it is clear that the Amendments may not be the meat on the plate but the whole meal of citizenship would not be complete without them. Historically, the players and events were varied and many. The main two participants in getting the Constitution ratified separated themselves between the Federalists and the Anti Federalists. Simply put it goes as follows: The Federalists wanted a strong central government. The Anti-Federalists wanted a central government too. They just wanted a strong pronouncement on States rights. The Federalists would make their case with the Federalists Papers. While consistently quoted in courts all across the United States, the Federalists Papers was a modern day equivalent of an op-ed piece in a major newspaper. It laid out an interpretation of the Constitution they had just written. The first ten Amendments, collectively known as the Bill of Rights spelled out specific rights and Federal Government limitations as to its power. Because of them you can freely talk shit about pretty much anything, worship any imaginary friend you want, get together with your friends and peacefully bitch about shit and you know, for the most part, the news you read is only half agenda induced bullshit.

The Bill of Rights allows you to carry a gun, shit! You are afforded a right to privacy and if you ever do do some foul shit you didn't do that foul shit until a dozen of your homies said you did. Oh, and even if your homies say your guilty your penance has to be proportional to the crime. Because of the Bill of Rights you can sue a motherfucker if you he tries to fuck you over. The highlight of the Bill of Rights is the Ninth Amendment. It reminds all Americans that even if a right isn't specifically mentioned you still have them. Like what choice of toothpaste you choose to use or what type of nail polish you wear.

The Eleventh Amendment lets the States fuck over non-resident citizens (and anyone else they so choose) through prosecutorial immunity. The Twelfth Amendment said that the Vice President of the United States is not automatically the first loser in the Presidential Election process.

The Thirteenth, Fourteenth and Fifteenth Amendments were all about Black folks. Known as the Reconstruction Amendments collectively, they ended and outlawed slavery (Thirteenth), granted full citizenship via "Equal Protection Clause" (Fourteenth), and the right to vote (Fifteenth). The Fourteenth Amendment would go on to be the foundation for many judicial arguments from its passage to present day.

The Sixteenth Amendment stipulated that yo ass will now pay income taxes.

The Seventeenth Amendment mandated that United States Senators now how to be elected by popular vote. They could no longer just be "picked" by their buddies.

The Eighteenth Amendment introduced Prohibition. This was a breakdown in the Constitutional machine. Of all the Amendments ratified this was the last ugly girl left at the club at two o'clock in the morning. But you fucked her anyway. By 1920 drinking alcohol was more than just a leisurely activity it was an involuntary function. Like your eyes blinking or your heart beating. An entire country succumbed to the whims of an idealistic few that not only pioneered, but mastered the art of lobbying.

The Nineteenth Amendment, like the Fifteenth Amendment before it and the Twenty-sixth after, cleared up further the "only White men" can vote bullshit. While the Fifteenth Amendment gave Blacks the vote, the Nineteenth Amendment would give Women the vote. The Twenty-sixth Amendment would later give the vote to eighteen year olds. It's ironically that all three Amendments dealing with the vote would take on lives. While women went through the shithole of citizen's rights because of sexism, once they got the vote, White men didn't fuck with them anymore about it, of course this only applied to White women. On the other hand the right to vote for Blacks was immediately eroded by States rights advocated using Jim Crow as a crowbar. With the ratification of the Nineteenth, Black women were lumped together with Black men and would not see full voting rights in the same way as ALL White people until well into the 1960s. One of the tools of that oppression, the poll tax, would require an Amendment in its own right to rectify (the Twenty-Fourth Amendment). None of this is the Author pontificating about the evils of White men. The fact of the matter is that the Sixty-sixth United States Congress was entirely made up of White males. No matter how any historian wants to slice up the facts no one can get around that truth. These men would oversee women getting the vote while, at the same time laying the foundation for marginalization of minorities for the next one hundred years and beyond. The Nineteenth Amendment is a clear example of the slow realization of "All men are created equal" in America.

The Twentieth Amendment mandated a new date when federally elected officials would begin work (from March to January). This was a nod to common sense and the Industrial Revolution. There was no need to delay America's business for four months while everyone made themselves to Washington, D.C.

The Twenty-first Amendment repealed the Eighteenth Amendment. Thank God. Cheers to that. It's important to note that the same fuckers that started the Twentieth Century Temperance movement would be one of the main advocates of repeal and the Twenty-First Amendment. The Twenty-First Amendment was also critical to Franklin Roosevelt's first Presidential Election victory in 1932. He simply promised a return of alcohol or what was referred to as supporting a "wet" platform. This was an important piece to what would become the beginning of the Roosevelt Monarchy (I mean Presidency).

The Twenty-second Amendment (because of the Roosevelt Monarchy) set term limits on how long a rich person can be President of the United States (now a maximum of eight years).

The Twenty-third Amendment gave Washington, D.C. residents voting participation in Presidential elections via the Electoral College. As a result the Democratic Party starts our every Presidential Election with three Electoral College votes.

As mentioned earlier the Twenty-Fourth Amendment eliminated the poll tax. The Amendment says that Black folks don't have pay for the right to vote. The legislation was part of a wave of civil rights measures to consume the Sixties.

The Twenty-fifth Amendment laid out the Presidential Line of Secession. Interestingly it also laid out the map on how to stage a coup d'état, or at least start a lot of shit in Washington, D.C.

The Twenty-sixth Amendment gave eighteen year olds the right to vote. 'Bout time. They are adults in every other aspect of life. Do you really think they can't choose among a group of liars to represent them just like everybody else? Exactly!

The Twenty-seventh Amendment mandates for the United States Congress that any pay raises can't take effect until the NEXT United States Congress takes office. What's interesting here is that the Twenty-seventh Amendment had a very long shelf life between inception, passage and ratification. Over two hundred years.

Of the six Amendments that came out of the United States Congress but failed to get State ratification, it the four that are still pending that represent Constitutional "loose ends."

Finally, as mentioned earlier the United States Constitution is by far a perfect document. But it good enough to make people from all over the world risk life and limb to get to America's shores. That fact alone is what makes America great. There are very few stories of boatloads of United States citizens rushing to see to get to Haiti. Or border patrol agents whining about the onslaught of American citizens trying to cross into Mexico. THAT is the legacy of the Amendments to the United States Constitution. This is what they mean when they call it "advanced citizenship!"

The end.

Bibliography

James J. Kilpatrick, ed. (1961). *The Constitution of the United States and Amendments Thereto*. ocrVirginia Commission on Constitutional Government. pp. 38, 63, 64.

James J. Kilpatrick, ed. (1961). *The Constitution of the United States and Amendments Thereto*. Virginia Commission on Constitutional Government. p. 65.

The 'Original' Thirteenth Amendment:The Misunderstood Titles of Nobility Amendment 94 Marquette Law Rev. 311 at 328, footnote 98 (fall 2001).

"The 'Original' Thirteenth Amendment: The Misunderstood Titles of Nobility Amendment". *Marquette Law Review* **94** (311). SSRN 1788908.

Dillon v. Gloss (1921) 256 U.S. 368 at 375, 65 L.Ed. 994 at 997, 41 S.Ct. 510 at 512.

Coleman v. Miller (1939) 307 U.S. 433 at 472, 83 L.Ed. 1385 at 1406, 59 S.Ct. 972 at 990 (dissenting op.)

Afroyim v. Rusk (1967) 387 U.S. 253 at 258-259 and 277-278, 18 L.Ed.2d 757 at 762 and 772, 87 S.Ct. 1660 at 1663 and 1673. *U.S. v. Tariq L. Belt*, Docket No. CIV- PJM-10-2921

State v. Casteel (Wis.App., July 31, 2001) 247 Wis.2d 451, 634 N.W.2d 338 at footnote 6.

- *The Abraham Lincoln Papers at the Library of Congress: Series 3. General Correspondence. 1837-1897*. Library of Congress.
- Adams, Les (1996). *The Second Amendment Primer: A Citizen's Guidebook to the History, Sources, and Authorities for the Constitutional Guarantee of the Right to Keep and Bear Arms*. Birmingham, Alabama: Paladium Press.
- Adamson, Barry (2008). *Freedom of Religion, the First Amendment, and the Supreme Court*. Pelican Publishing. ISBN 1-58980-520-8.
- Anderson, Casey; Horwitz, Joshua (2009). *Guns, Democracy, and the Insurrectionist Idea*. Ann Arbor, MI: University of Michigan Press.ISBN 0-472-03370-0.
- Barnett, Hilaire (2004). *Constitutional & Administrative Law*. Routledge Cavendish. ISBN 1-85941-927-5.
- Bickford, Charlene; et al., eds. (2004). *Documentary History of the First Federal Congress of the United States of America, March 4, 1789 – March 3, 1791: Correspondence: First Session, September–November 1789* **17**. The Johns Hopkins University Press. ISBN 978-0-8018-7162-7.
- Bogus, Carl T. (2001). *The Second Amendment in Law and History: Historians and Constitutional Scholars on the Right to Bear Arms*. New York: The New Press. ISBN 1-56584-699-0.
- Boynton, Lindsay Oliver J. (1971). *The Elizabethan Militia 1558–1638*. David & Charles. ISBN 0-7153-5244-X. OCLC 8605166.

- Carter, Gregg Lee (2002). *Guns in American Society.* ABC-CLIO.

- Charles, Patrick J. (2009). *The Second Amendment: The Intent and Its Interpretation by the States and the Supreme Court.* McFarland.ISBN 978-0-7864-4270-6.

- Cooke, Edward Francis (2002). *A Detailed Analysis of the Constitution.* Lanham, MD: Rowman & Littlefield Publishers. ISBN 0-7425-2238-5.

- Cornell, Saul (2006). *A Well-Regulated Militia — The Founding Fathers and the Origins of Gun Control in America.* New York, New York: Oxford University Press. ISBN 978-0-19-514786-5.

- Cottrol, Robert (1994). *Gun Control and the Constitution: Sources and Explorations on the Second Amendment.* Taylor & Francis.

- Cramer, Clayton E.; Olson, Joseph (2008). "What Did "Bear Arms" Mean in the Second Amendment?". *Geo. J.L. & Pub. Pol'y* **6** (2).

- Crooker, Constance Emerson (2003). *Gun Control and Gun Rights.* Greenwood Publishing Group. ISBN 978-0-313-32174-0.

- Denson, John V. (1999). *The Costs of War: America's Pyrrhic Victories*(2 ed.). Transaction Publishers. ISBN 978-0-7658-0487-7.

- Doherty, Brian (2008). *Gun Control on Trial: Inside the Supreme Court Battle Over the Second Amendment.* Washington, D.C.: Cato Institute.ISBN 1-933995-25-4.

- Dulaney, W. Marvin (1996). *Black Police in America.* Bloomington: Indiana University Press. ISBN 0-253-21040-2.

- Ely, James W.; Bodenhamer, David J. (2008). *The Bill of Rights in Modern America.* Bloomington: Indiana University Press. ISBN 0-253-21991-4.

- Foner, Eric; Garraty, John Arthur (1991). *The Reader's Companion to American History.* Houghton Mifflin Harcourt. ISBN 0-395-51372-3.

- Frey, Raymond; Wellman, Christopher (2003). *A Companion to Applied Ethics*. Cambridge, MA: Blackwell Publishing. ISBN 1-55786-594-9.

- Halbrook, Stephen P. (1989). *A Right to Bear Arms: State and Federal Bills of Rights and Constitutional Guarantees*. Greenwood Publishing Group.

- Halbrook, Stephen P. (1994). *That Every Man Be Armed: The Evolution of a Constitutional Right (Independent Studies in Political Economy)*. Oakland, CA: The Independent Institute. ISBN 0-945999-38-0.

- Hemenway, David (2007). *Private Guns, Public Health*. University of Michigan Press. ISBN 978-0-472-03162-7.

- Kruschke, Earl R. (1995). *Gun Control: A Reference Handbook*. Santa Barbara, CA: ABC-CLIO. ISBN 0-87436-695-X.

- Levy, Leonard W. (1999). *Origins of the Bill of Rights*. New Haven, CT: Yale University Press. ISBN 0-300-07802-1.

- Madison, James (2010). *The Writings of James Madison: 1787–1790*. Nabu Press. ISBN 978-1-144-58273-7.

- Malcolm, Joyce Lee (1996). *To Keep and Bear Arms: The Origins of an Anglo-American Right*. Cambridge: Harvard University Press. ISBN 0-674-89307-7.

- Merkel, William G.; Uviller, H. Richard (2002). *The Militia and the Right to Arms, Or, How the Second Amendment Fell Silent*. Durham, NC: Duke University Press. ISBN 0-8223-3017-2. Retrieved February 14,2013.

- Millis, Walter (1981). *Arms and Men*. Rutgers University Press.

- Mulloy, D. (2004). *American Extremism*. Routledge.

- Pepper, John; Petrie, Carol; Wellford, Charles F. (2005). *Firearms and Violence. A Critical Review*. Washington, DC: National Academies Press. ISBN 0-309-09124-1.

- Pole, J. R.; Greene, Jack P. (2003). *A Companion to the American Revolution (Blackwell Companions to American History)*. Cambridge, MA: Blackwell Publishers. ISBN 1-4051-1674-9.

- Renehan, Edward J. (1997). *The Secret Six: The True Tale of the Men Who Conspired With John Brown*. Columbia, SC: University of South Carolina Press. ISBN 1-57003-181-9.

- Schmidt, Steffen; Bardes, Barbara A.; Shelley, Mack C. (2008). *American Government and Politics Today: The Essentials*. Belmont, CA: Wadsworth Publishing. ISBN 0-495-57170-9.

- Shapiro, Ilya (2008). *Cato Supreme Court Review 2007–2008*. Washington, D.C: Cato Institute. ISBN 1-933995-17-3.

- Smith, Rich (2007). *The Bill of Rights: Defining Our Freedoms*. ABDO Group. ISBN 978-1-59928-913-7.

- Spitzer, Robert J. (2001). *The Right to Bear Arms: Rights and Liberties under the Law*. Santa Barbara, CA: ABC-CLIO. ISBN 1-57607-347-5.

- Szatmary, David P. (1980). *Shays' Rebellion: the Making of an Agrarian Insurrection*. Amherst: University of Massachusetts Press. ISBN 0-87023-295-9.

- Tucker, St. George; Blackstone, William (1996). *Blackstone's Commentaries: With Notes of Reference to the Constitution and Laws, of the Federal Government of the United States, and of the Commonwealth of Virginia: In Five Volumes*. The Lawbook Exchange, Ltd. ISBN 978-1-886363-15-1.

- Tushnet, Mark V. (2007). *Out of Range: Why the Constitution Can't End the Battle Over Guns.* Oxford University Press. pp. xv. ISBN 978-0-19-530424-4.

- Rabban, David (1999). *Free Speech in its Forgotten Years.* Cambridge University Press.

- Rawle, William (1829). *A View of the Constitution of the United States of America* (2 ed.). P.H. Nicklin.

- Spooner, Lysander (1852). *An Essay on the Trial by Jury.* RetrievedJuly 6, 2013.

- Vile, John R. (2005). *The Constitutional Convention of 1787: A Comprehensive Encyclopedia of America's Founding (2 Volume Set).* Santa Barbara, CA: ABC-CLIO. ISBN 1-85109-669-8.

- Williams, David H. (2003). *The Mythic Meanings of the Second Amendment: Taming Political Violence in a Constitutional Republic.* New Haven, CT: Yale University Press. ISBN 0-300-09562-7.

- Wills, Garry (2000). Saul, Cornell, ed. *Whose Right to Bear Arms did the Second Amendment Protect?.* Boston: Bedford/St. Martin's. ISBN 0-312-24060-0.

- Wills, Garry (2002). *A Necessary Evil: A History of American Distrust of Government.* New York: Simon & Schuster. pp. 256–7. ISBN 0-684-87026-6.

- Winterer, Caroline (2002). *The Culture of Classicism: Ancient Greece and Rome in American Intellectual Life, 1780–1910.* Baltimore: Johns Hopkins University Press.

- Young, David E. (2001). *The Origin of the Second Amendment: A Documentary History of the Bill of Rights 1787–1792* (2 ed.). Golden Oak Books. ISBN 0-9623664-3-9.

Barnett, Gary E. (June 24, 2008). "The Reasonable Regulation of the Right to Keep and Bear Arms". *Geo. J.L. & Pub. Pol'y* **6** (2).

- Bogus, Carl (1998). "The Hidden History of the Second Amendment".*U.C. Davis L. Rev.* **31**.
- Blodgett-Ford, Sayoko (Fall 1995). "The Changing Meaning of the Right to Bear Arms". *Seton Hall Const. L.J.* **101**.
- Breen, T. H. (1972). "English Origins and New World Development: The Case of the Covenanted Militia in Seventeenth-Century Massachusetts". *Past & Present* **57** (1): 74.doi:10.1093/past/57.1.74.
- Sunstein, Cass (November 2008). "Comment: Second Amendment Minimalism: Heller as Griswold". *Harv. L. Rev.* **122**. RetrievedFebruary 20, 2009.
- Charles, Patrick J. (2009). "'Arms for Their Defence?': An Historical, Legal, and Textual Analysis of the English Right to Have Arms and Whether the Second Amendment should Be Incorporated in McDonald v. City of Chicago". *Clev. St. L. Rev.* **57** (3).
- Cramer, Clayton (Winter 1995). "The Racist Roots of Gun Control".*Kan. J. Of Pub. Pol'y*.
- Davies, Ross (Winter 2008). "Which is the Constitution" (PDF). *Green Bag 2d* **11** (2): 209–16.
- Gunn, Steven H. (1998). "A Lawyer's Guide to the Second Amendment".*BYU L. Rev.* **35**.
- Hardy, David (2007). "Book Review: A Well-Regulated Militia: The Founding Fathers and the Origins of Gun Control in America". *Wm. & Mary Bill of Rts. J.* **15**.

- Henigan, Denis (1991). "Arms, Anarchy, and the Second Amendment". *Val. L. Rev.* **26** (107).*dead link*
- Heyman, Stephen (2000). "Natural Rights and the Second Amendment". *Chi.-Kent. L. Rev.* **76** (237).
- Kates, Jr., Don B. (November 1983). "Handgun Prohibition and the Original Meaning of the Second Amendment". *Mich. L. Rev.* (Michigan Law Review, Vol. 82, No. 2) **82** (2): 204–273. doi:10.2307/1288537.JSTOR 1288537.
- Konig, David Thomas (2004). "The Second Amendment: A Missing Transatlantic Context for the Historical Meaning of "the Right of the People to Keep and Bear Arms"". *Law and History Review* **22** (1).
- Lund, Nelson. "Heller and Second Amendment Precedent". *Lewis & Clark L. Rev.*
- Malcolm, Joyce Lee (1986). "Book Review: That Every Man Be Armed"**54**.
- Malcolm, Joyce Lee (1993). "The Role of the Militia in the Development of the Englishman's Right to be Armed — Clarifying the Legacy". *J. On Firearms & Pub. Pol'y* **5**.
- McAffee, Thomas B.; Quinlan, Michael J. (March 1997). "Bringing Forward the Right to Keep and Bear Arms: Do Text, History, or Precedent Stand in the Way?". *N.C. L. Rev.*
- McClurg, Andrew (1999). "Lotts' More Guns and Other Fallacies Infecting the Gun Control Debate". *J. Of Firearms & Pub. Pol'y* **11**.
- Merkel, William (Summer 2009). "Heller and Scalia's Originalism"(PDF). *Lewis & Clark L. Rev.* **13** (2).
- Pierce, Darell R. (1982). "Second Amendment Survey". *N. Ky. L. Rev.* **10** (1).

- Rakove, Jack (2000). "The Second Amendment: The Highest Stage of Originalism". *Chi.-Kent. L. Rev.* **76**.
- Reynolds, Glenn (1995). "A Critical Guide to the Second Amendment". *Tenn. L. Rev.* **62** (461).
- Schmidt, Christopher (February 2007). "An International Human Right to Keep and Bear Arms". *Wm. & Mary Bill of Rts. J.* **15** (3): 983.
- Smith, Douglas (2008). "The Second Amendment and the Supreme Court". *Geo. J.L. & Pub. Pol'y* **6**.
- Volokh, Eugene (1998). "The Commonplace Second Amendment".*NYU L. Rev.* **73** (793).
- Volokh, Eugene (November–December 1998). "Testimony of Eugene Volokh on the Second Amendment, Senate Subcommittee on the Constitution, September 23, 1998". *Cal. Pol. Rev.*
- Weisselberg, Charles D. (2009). "Selected Criminal Law Cases in the Supreme Court's 2007–2008 Term, and a Look Ahead" (PDF). *Court Review* **44**.
- Wills, Garry (1995). "To Keep and Bear Arms". *N.Y. Rev. Of Books* **42** (14). ISSN 0028-7504.
- Winkler, Adam (February 2007). "Scrutinizing the Second Amendment".*Mich. L. Rev.* **105**.
- Winkler, Adam (June 2009). "Heller's Catch 22". *UCLA L. Rev.* **56**.SSRN 1359225.
- Alderman, Ellen and Caroline Kennedy (1991). *In Our Defense.* Avon.
- Amar, Akhil Reed (1998). *The Bill of Rights.* Yale University Press.
- Beeman, Richard (2009). *Plain, Honest Men: The Making of the American Constitution.* Random House.

- Bell, Tom W. (1993) "The Third Amendment: Forgotten but Not Gone". *William & Mary Bill of Rights Journal* 2.1: pp. 117–150.

- Labunski, Richard E. (2006). *James Madison and the struggle for the Bill of Rights*. Oxford University Press.

- Wood, Gordon S. (2009). *Empire of Liberty: A History of the Early Republic, 1789–1815*. Oxford University Press.

- Adams, Charles Francis; Adams, John (1856). *The Works of John Adams, Second President of the United States: With a Life of the Author*. Vol. 1 publisher=Little, Brown.

- Beeman, Richard (2009). *Plain, Honest Men: The Making of the American Constitution*. Random House.

- Crisera, Maria Lisa (1990). "Reevaluation of the California Corpus Delicti Rule: A Response to the Invitation of Proposition 8". *California Law Review* **78** (6).

- Davies, Thomas Y. (1999). "Recovering the Original Fourth Amendment". *Michigan Law Review* **98** (3): 547–750. doi:10.2307/1290314. JSTOR 1290314.

- Kilman, Johnny; Costello, George, eds. (2006). *The Constitution of the United States of America: Analysis and Interpretation*. GPO.

- Labunski, Richard E. (2006). *James Madison and the struggle for the Bill of Rights*. Oxford University Press.

- Lasson, Nelson B. (1937). *The History and Development of the Fourth Amendment to the United States Constitution*. Johns Hopkins University Press.

- Levy, Leonard Williams (1995). *Seasoned Judgments: The American Constitution, Rights, and History*. Transaction Publishers.

- Maier, Pauline (2010). *Ratification: The People Debate the Constitution, 1787–1788*. Simon and Schuster.

- Wood, Gordon S. (2009). *Empire of Liberty: A History of the Early Republic, 1789–1815*. Oxford University Press.
- Wroth, Kinvin; Zobel, Hiller B., eds. (1965). *Legal Papers of John Adams*. Vol. 2. Belknap Press.
- *Ex parte Wilson*, 114 U.S. 417 (1885)

Harper, Timothy (October 2, 2007). *The Complete Idiot's Guide to the U.S. Constitution*. Penguin Group. p. 109. ISBN 978-1-59257-627-2. However, the Fifth Amendment contains several other important provisions for protecting your rights. It is the source of the double jeopardy doctrine, which prevents authorities from trying a person twice for the same crime ...

Greaves, Richard L. (1981). "Legal Problems". *Society and religion in Elizabethan England*. Minneapolis, Minnesota:University of Minnesota Press. pp. 649, 681. ISBN 0-8166-1030-4.OCLC 7278140. Retrieved 19 July 2009. This situation worsened in the 1580s and 1590s when the machinery of ... the High Commission, was turned against Puritans ... in which a key weapon was the oath *ex officio mero*, with its capacity for self incrimination ... Refusal to take this oath usually was regarded as proof of guilt.

Michael J. Z. Mannheimer, "Ripeness of Self-Incrimination Clause Disputes," *Journal of Criminal Law and Criminology*, Vol. 95, No. 4, p. 1261, footnote 1 (Northwestern Univ. School of Law 2005), citing*Malloy v. Hogan*, 378 U.S. 1 (1964)).

Miniter, Frank (2011). *Saving the Bill of Rights: Exposing the Left's Campaign to Destroy American Exceptionalism*. Regnery Publishing. p. 204. ISBN 978-1-59698-150-8.

- Amar, Akhil Reed; Lettow, Renée B. (1995). "Fifth Amendment First Principles: The Self-Incrimination Clause". *Michigan Law Review* (The Michigan Law Review Association) **93** (5): 857–928. doi:10.2307/1289986. JSTOR 1289986.

- Davies, Thomas Y. (2003). "Farther and Farther From the Original Fifth Amendment" (PDF). *Tennessee Law Review* (70): 987–1045. Retrieved 2010-04-06.

- Baicker-McKee, Steven; William M. Janssen; and John B. Corr (2008) [1997]. *A Student's Guide to the Federal Rules of Civil Procedure.* Thomson West.

- Beeman, Richard (2009). *Plain, Honest Men: The Making of the American Constitution.* Random House.

- Labunski, Richard E. (2006). *James Madison and the struggle for the Bill of Rights.* Oxford University Press.

- Levy, Leonard Williams (1995). *Seasoned Judgments: The American Constitution, Rights, and History.* Transaction Publishers.

- Maier, Pauline (2010). *Ratification: The People Debate the Constitution, 1787–1788.* Simon and Schuster.

- Wolfram, Charles W. (1973). "The Constitutional History of the Seventh Amendment", 57 *Minnesota Law Review* 639, 670-71.

- Barnett, Randy E. (2005). *Restoring the Lost Constitution: The Presumption of Liberty.* Princeton, NJ: Princeton University Press. ISBN 0-691-12376-4.

- Farber, Daniel A. (2007). *Retained by the People: The "Silent" Ninth Amendment and the Constitutional Rights Americans Don't Know They Have.* Perseus Books Group. ISBN 0-465-02298-7.

- Lash, Kurt T. (2009). *The Lost History of the Ninth Amendment.* Oxford University Press. ISBN 0-19-537261-1.

- Belz, Herman. *Emancipation and Equal Rights: Politics and Constitutionalism in the Civil War Era* (1978) online

- Benedict, Michael Les. "Constitutional Politics, Constitutional Law, and the Thirteenth Amendment". *Maryland Law Review* 71 (1), October 31, 2012.

- Blackmon, Douglas A. (March 25, 2008). *Slavery by Another Name: The Re-Enslavement of Black Americans from the Civil War to World War II*. Knopf Doubleday Publishing Group.ISBN 978-0-385-50625-0.

- Colbert, Douglas L. "Liberating the Thirteenth Amendment", *Harvard Civil Rights – Civil Liberties Law Review* 30, 1995; pp. 1 – 55.

- Cramer, Clayton E. (1997). *Black Demographic Data, 1790-1860: A Sourcebook*. Greenwood Publishing Group. ISBN 9780313302435.

- Donald, David Herbert (1996). *Lincoln*. Simon & Schuster. ISBN 978-0-684-82535-9. RetrievedJune 5, 2013.

- Du Bois, W.E.B. (1935). *Black Reconstruction: An Essay Toward a History of the Part Which Black Folk Played in the Attempt to Reconstruct Democracy in America, 1860–1880'*. New York: Russell & Russell.

- Foner, Eric (2010). *The Fiery Trial: Abraham Lincoln and American Slavery*. W. W. Norton.ISBN 978-0-393-06618-0. Retrieved June 4, 2013.

- Forehand, Beverly (1996). *Striking Resemblance: Kentucky, Tennessee, Black Codes and Readjustment, 1865–1866*. Western Kentucky University, Masters Thesis.

- Goluboff, Risa L. "The Thirteenth Amendment and the Lost Origins of Civil Rights". *Duke Law Journal* 50, 2001; pp. 1609–1685.

- Goldstone, Lawrence (2011). *Inherently Unequal: The Betrayal of Equal Rights by the Supreme Court, 1865-1903*. Walker & Company. ISBN 978-0-8027-1792-4.

- Goodwin, Doris Kearns (2005). *Team of Rivals: The Political Genius of Abraham Lincoln*. Simon & Schuster. ISBN 978-0-7432-7075-5. Retrieved June 2, 2013.

- Harrison, John. "The Lawfulness of the Reconstruction Amendments". *University of Chicago Law Review* 68 (2); Spring, 2001; pp. 375–462. in JStor

- Kachun, Mitch. *Festivals of Freedom: Memory and Meaning in African American Emancipation Celebrations, 1808–1915* (2003) online

- McAward, Jennifer Mason. "McCulloch and the Thirteenth Amendment", *Columbia Law Review* 112, 2012, pp. 1769–1809.

- McPherson, James M. (1988). *Battle Cry of Freedom: The Civil War Era*. Oxford University Press. ISBN 978-0-19-503863-7. Retrieved June 5, 2013.

- Novak, Daniel A. *The Wheel of Servitude: Black Forced Labor after Slavery*. University Press of Kentucky, 1978. ISBN 0813113717

- Richards, Leonard L. *Who Freed the Slaves?: The Fight over the Thirteenth Amendment* (2015)excerpt; emphasis on the role of Congressman James Ashley

- Stanley, Amy Dru. "Instead of Waiting for the Thirteenth Amendment: The War Power, Slave Marriage, and Inviolate Human Rights". *American Historical Review 113 (3), June 2010; pp. 732 –765.*

- Stromberg, Joseph R. "A Plain Folk Perspective on Reconstruction, State-Building, Ideology, and Economic Spoils". *Journal of Libertarian Studies* 16 (2), Spring 2002; pp. 103–137.

- TenBroek, Jacobus. "Thirteenth Amendment to the Constitution of the United States: Consummation to Abolition and Key to the Fourteenth Amendment". *California Law Review* 39 (2), June 1951; pp. 171–203.

- Thorpe, Francis Newton. *The Constitutional History of the United States, vol. 3: 1861 – 1895.* Chicago: Callaghan, 1901.

- Trelease, Allen W. *White Terror: The Ku Klux Klan Conspiracy and Southern Reconstruction.* New York: Harper & Row, 1971. ISBN

- Tsesis, Alexander. *The Thirteenth Amendment and American Freedom: A Legal History.* New York University Press, 2004. ISBN 0814782760

- Vicino, Thomas J.; Hanlon, Bernadette (2014). *Global Migration The Basics.* Routledge, 190 pages. ISBN 9781134696871.

- Vorenberg, Michael. *Final Freedom: The Civil War, the Abolition of Slavery, and the Thirteenth Amendment.* Cambridge University Press, 2001. ISBN 9781139428002

- Wolff, Tobias Barrington. "The Thirteenth Amendment and Slavery in the Global Economy".*Columbia Law Review* 102(4); May 2002; pp. 973–1050.

- Wood, Gordon S (2010). *Empire of Liberty: A History of the Early Republic, 1789–1815.*

- Oxford University Press. ISBN 978-0-19-503914-6., Book

- Foner, Eric (1988). *Reconstruction: America's Unfinished Revolution, 1863-1877.* HarperCollins. ISBN 978-0-06-203586-8.

- Goldstone, Lawrence (2011). *Inherently Unequal: The Betrayal of Equal Rights by the Supreme Court, 1865-1903.* Walker & Company. ISBN 978-0-8027-1792-4.

- Graber, Mark A. "Subtraction by Addition? The Thirteenth and Fourteenth Amendments". *Columbia Law Review* 112(7), November 2012; pp. 1501–1549.

- Soifer, Aviam. "Federal Protection, Paternalism, and the Virtually Forgotten Prohibition of Voluntary Peonage". *Columbia Law Review* 112(7), November 2012; pp. 1607–1640.

- Halbrook, Stephen P. (1998). *Freedmen, the 14th Amendment, and the Right to Bear Arms, 1866-1876.* Greenwood Publishing Group. ISBN 9780275963316. Retrieved March 29, 2013. at Questia

- Bogen, David S. (April 30, 2003). *Privileges and Immunities: A Reference Guide to the United States Constitution.* Greenwood Publishing Group. ISBN 9780313313479. Retrieved March 19, 2013.

- Gillette, William (1965). *The Right to Vote: Politics and the Passage of the Fifteenth Amendment.* Johns Hopkins Press.

- Goldman, Robert Michael (2001). *A Free Ballot and a Fair Count: The Department of Justice and the Enforcement of Voting Rights in the South, 1877–1893.* Fordham Univ Press. ISBN 978-0-8232-2084-7.

- Johnson, Paul (2000). *A History of the American People.* Orion Publishing Group, Limited. ISBN 978-1-84212-425-3.

- Palumbo, Arthur E. (2009). *The Authentic Constitution: An Originalist View of America's Legacy.* Algora Publishing. ISBN 978-0-87586-707-6.

- Stromberg, Joseph R. "A Plain Folk Perspective on Reconstruction, State-Building, Ideology, and Economic Spoils". *Journal of Libertarian Studies* 16 (2), Spring 2002; pp. 103–137.

- Amar, Vikram David (2008). "Are Statutes Constraining Gubernatorial Power to Make Temporary Appointments to the United States Senate Constitutional Under the Seventeenth

Amendment?".*Hastings Constitutional Law Quarterly* (University of California, Hastings College of the Law) **35** (4). ISSN 0094-5617.

- Bybee, Jay S. (1997). "Ulysses at the Mast: Democracy, Federalism, and the Sirens' Song of the Seventeenth Amendment". *Northwestern University Law Review* (Northwestern University School of Law) **91** (1). ISSN 0029-3571.

- Gold, Kevin M. (1992). "Trinsey v. Pennsylvania: State Discretion to Regulate United States Senate Vacancy". *Widener Journal of Law and Public Policy* (Widener University School of Law) **2** (1). ISSN 1064-5012.

- Hoebeke, Christopher Hyde (1995). *The road to mass democracy: original intent and the Seventeenth Amendment.* Transaction Publishers. ISBN 1-56000-217-4.

- Kochan, Donald J. (2003). "State Laws and the Independent Judiciary: An Analysis of the Effects of the Seventeenth Amendment on the Number of Supreme Court Cases Holding State Laws Unconstitutional". *Albany Law Review* **66** (1). ISSN 0002-4678.

- Levinson, Sanford (2008). "Political Party and Senatorial Succession: A Response to Vikram Amar on How Best to Interpret the Seventeenth Amendment". *Hastings Constitutional Law Quarterly*(University of California, Hastings College of the Law) **35** (4). ISSN 0094-5617.

- Novakovic, Michael B. (1992). "Constitutional Law: Filling Senate Vacancies". *Villanova Law Review* (Villanova University School of Law) **37** (1). ISSN 0042-6229.

- Riker, William H. (1955). "The Senate and American Federalism". *American Political Science Review* (American Political Science Association) **49** (2). ISSN 0003-0554.

- Rossum, Ralph A. (1999). "The Irony of Constitutional Democracy: Federalism, the Supreme Court, and the Seventeenth Amendment". *San Diego Law Review* (University of San Diego School of Law)**36** (3). ISSN 0886-3210.

- Tushnet, Mark (2010). *The Constitution of the United States of America: A Contextual Analysis.* Hart Publishing. ISBN 978-1-84113-738-4.

- Ure, James Christian (2007). "You Scratch My Back and I'll Scratch Yours: Why the Federal Marriage Amendment Should Also Repeal the Seventeenth Amendment". *South Texas Law Review* (South Texas College of Law) **49** (1). ISSN 1052-343X.

- Vile, John R. (2003). *Encyclopedia of constitutional amendments, proposed amendments, and amending issues, 1789–2002* (2nd ed.). ABC-CLIO. ISBN 978-1-85109-428-8.

- Vile, John R. (2010). *A companion to the United States Constitution and its amendments* (5th ed.). ABC-CLIO. ISBN 978-0-313-38008-2.

- Zywicki, Todd J. (1994). "Senators and Special Interests: A Public Choice Analysis of the Seventeenth Amendment" (PDF). *Oregon Law Review* (University of Oregon School of Law) **73** (1).ISSN 0196-2043.

- Zywicki, Todd J. (1997). "Beyond the Shell and Husk of History: The History of the Seventeenth Amendment and its Implications for Current Reform Proposals" (PDF). *Cleveland State Law Review*(Cleveland-Marshall College of Law) **45** (1). ISSN 0009-8876.

- Amar, Akhil Reed (2005). *America's Constitution: A Biography.* Random House trade pbk. ed. ISBN 0-8129-7272-4.

- Anzalone, Christopher A (2002). *Supreme Court Cases on Gender and Sexual Equality, 1787–2001.* United States Supreme Court (Sharpe). ISBN 0-7656-0683-6.

- Baker, Jean H. (ed.) (2002). *Votes for Women: The Struggle for Suffrage Revisited*. Oxford University Press. ISBN 978-0-19-802983-0.

- Banaszak, Lee A. (1996). *Why Movements Succeed or Fail: Opportunity, Culture, and the Struggle for Woman Suffrage*. Princeton University Press. ISBN 978-1-4008-2207-2.

- DuBois, Ellen C., Ellen C. (1998). *Woman Suffrage & Women's Rights*. NYU Press. ISBN 978-0-8147-1900-8.

- Dumenil, Lynn (1995). *The Modern Temper: American Culture and Society in the 1920s*. Hill and Wang. ISBN 0-8090-6978-4.

- Hakim, Joy (1995). "Book 9: War, Peace, and All That Jazz". *A History of US*. New York, New York: Oxford University Press. ISBN 0-19-509514-6.

- Flexner, Eleanor (1959). *Century of Struggle*. Cambridge, MA: Belknap Press of Harvard University. ISBN 978-0674106536.

- Mead, Rebecca J. (2004). *How the Vote Was Won: Woman Suffrage in the Western United States, 1868–1914*. NYU Press. ISBN 978-0-8147-5676-8.

- Moses, Claire Goldberg; Hartmann, Heidi I. (1995). *U.S. Women in Struggle: A Feminist Studies Anthology*. University of Illinois Press. ISBN 0-252-02166-5.

- Van West, Carroll (ed.) (1998). "Woman Suffrage Movement". *Tennessee Encyclopedia of History and Culture*. Tennessee Historical Society. ISBN 1-55853-599-3.

- Wheeler, Marjorie S. (1993). *New Women of the New South: The Leaders of the Woman Suffrage Movement in the Southern States*. Oxford University Press. ISBN 978-0-19-535957-2.

- Stansell, Christine (2011). *The Feminist Promise*. The Modern Library. ISBN 9781588369161.

- *Constitution of the United States.*

- Kilman, Johnny and George Costello (Eds). (2000). *The Constitution of the United States of America: Analysis and Interpretation.*

- Vose, Clement (1978). "When District of Columbia Representation Collides with the Constitutional Amendment Institution". *Publius* (Oxford University Press) **9** (1): 105–125. doi:10.2307/3329772. Retrieved February 1, 2013.

- Lawson, Steven F. (1976). *Black Ballots: Voting Rights in the South, 1944-1969.* New York: Columbia University Press.

- Ogden, Frederic D. (1958). *The Poll Tax in the South.* University of Alabama Press.

- *One Heartbeat Away* by Birch Bayh (1968).

- CNN Transcript of White House press briefing re G.W. Bush temporary transfer of power to VP Cheney June 29, 2002 (URL accessed June 4, 2006).

- CNN Story of White House statement regarding G.W. Bush temporary transfer of power to VP Cheney July 21, 2007.

- *The Twenty-Fifth Amendment: Its Complete History and Applications* by John Feerick (1992).

- *Presidential Inability and the Twenty-Fifth Amendment's Unexplored Removal Provisions* by Scott Gant, Michigan State Law Review (1999), p. 791.

- *Presidential Inability and Subjective Meaning* by Adam R. F. Gustafson, Yale Law & Policy Review, Vol. 27 (2009), p. 459.

- Bryant, A. Christopher (2003). "Stopping Time: The Pro-Slavery and 'Irrevocable' Thirteenth Amendment". *Harvard Journal of Law and Public Policy* **26**: 501. ISSN 0193-4872.

- Lee, R. Alton (1961). "The Corwin Amendment in the Secession Crisis". *The Ohio Historical Quarterly* **70** (1): 1–26.

- Martin, Philip E. (1966). "Illinois' Ratification of the Corwin Amendment". *Journal of Public Law* **15**: 18–91.

- Baldez, Lisa; Epstein, Lee; Martin, Andrew D. (2006). "Does the U.S. Constitution Need an Equal Rights Amendment?". *Journal of Legal Studies* **35** (1): 243–283. doi:10.1086/498836.

- Bradley, Martha S. (2005). *Pedestals and Podiums: Utah Women, Religious Authority, and Equal Rights.* Salt Lake City, UT: Signature Books. ISBN 1-56085-189-9.

- Critchlow, Donald T. (2005). *Phyllis Schlafly and Grassroots Conservatism: A Woman's Crusade.* Princeton, NJ: Princeton University Press. ISBN 0-691-07002-4.

- Critchlow, Donald T., and Stachecki, Cynthia L. (2008). "The Equal Rights Amendment Reconsidered: Politics, Policy, and Social Mobilization in a Democracy," *Journal of Policy History* Volume 20, Number 1 online

- Dunlap, Mary C. (1976) "The Equal Rights Amendment and the Courts." *Pepperdine Law Review* Volume 3, Number 1 online

- Hatch, Orrin G. (1983). *The Equal Rights Amendment: Myths and Realities*, Savant Press. Library of Congress permalink

- Lee, Rex E. (1980). *A Lawyer Looks at the Equal Rights Amendment.* Provo, UT: Brigham Young University Press. ISBN 0-8425-1883-5.

- Kempker, Erin M. (2013) "Coalition and Control: Hoosier Feminists and the Equal Rights Amendment." *Frontiers: A Journal of Women Studies* 34.2 (2013): 52-82. online

- Mansbridge, Jane J. (1986). *Why We Lost the ERA.* Chicago: University of Chicago Press. ISBN 0-226-50358-5.

- Neale, T. H. (2013). *The proposed Equal Rights Amendment: Contemporary ratification issues* (Washington, DC: Congressional Research Service) online

- McBride, Genevieve G. (2005). "'Forward' Women: Winning the Wisconsin Campaign for the Country's First ERA, 1921.". In Peter Watson Boone (ed.). *The Quest for Social Justice III*. Milwaukee, WI: UW-Milwaukee. ISBN 1-879281-26-0.

- Meyerson, Michael I. *Liberty's Blueprint: How Madison and Hamilton Wrote the Federalist Papers, Defined the Constitution, and Made Democracy Safe for the World*, New York: Basic Books, 2008.

- Dietze, Gottfried. *The Federalist: A Classic on Federalism and Free Government*, Baltimore: The Johns Hopkins Press, 1960.

- Epstein, David F. *The Political Theory of the Federalist*, Chicago: The University of Chicago Press, 1984.

- Gray, Leslie, and Wynell Burroughs. "Teaching With Documents: Ratification of the Constitution", *Social Education*, 51 (1987): 322-324.

- Kesler, Charles R. *Saving the Revolution: The Federalist Papers and the American Founding*, New York: 1987.

- Patrick, John J., and Clair W. Keller. *Lessons on the Federalist Papers: Supplements to High School Courses in American History, Government and Civics*, Bloomington, IN: Organization of American Historians in association with ERIC/ChESS, 1987. ED 280 764.

- Schechter, Stephen L. *Teaching about American Federal Democracy*, Philadelphia: Center for the Study of Federalism at Temple University, 1984. ED 248 161.

- Scott, Kyle. *The Federalist Papers: A Reader's Guide* (New York: Bloomsbury Press, 2013) 202 pp.

- Sunstein, Cass R. *The Enlarged Republic—Then and Now*, New York Review of Books, (March 26, 2009): Volume LVI, Number 5, 45. http://www.nybooks.com/articles/22453

- Webster, Mary E. *The Federalist Papers: In Modern Language Indexed for Today's Political Issues.* Bellevue, WA.: Merril Press, 1999.

- White, Morton. *Philosophy, The Federalist, and the Constitution,* New York: 1987.

- Zebra Edition. *The Federalist Papers: (Or, How Government is Supposed to Work), Edited for Readability.* Oakesdale, WA: Lucky Zebra Press, 2007.

- Meyerson, Michael I. *Liberty's Blueprint: How Madison and Hamilton Wrote the Federalist Papers, Defined the Constitution, and Made Democracy Safe for the World,* New York: Basic Books, 2008.

- Dietze, Gottfried. *The Federalist: A Classic on Federalism and Free Government,* Baltimore: The Johns Hopkins Press, 1960.

- Epstein, David F. *The Political Theory of the Federalist,* Chicago: The University of Chicago Press, 1984.

- Gray, Leslie, and Wynell Burroughs. "Teaching With Documents: Ratification of the Constitution", *Social Education,* 51 (1987): 322-324.

- Kesler, Charles R. *Saving the Revolution: The Federalist Papers and the American Founding,* New York: 1987.

- Patrick, John J., and Clair W. Keller. *Lessons on the Federalist Papers: Supplements to High School Courses in American History, Government and Civics,* Bloomington, IN: Organization of American Historians in association with ERIC/ChESS, 1987. ED 280 764.

- Schechter, Stephen L. *Teaching about American Federal Democracy,* Philadelphia: Center for the Study of Federalism at Temple University, 1984. ED 248 161.

- Scott, Kyle. *The Federalist Papers: A Reader's Guide* (New York: Bloomsbury Press, 2013) 202 pp.

- Sunstein, Cass R. *The Enlarged Republic—Then and Now*, New York Review of Books, (March 26, 2009): Volume LVI, Number 5, 45. http://www.nybooks.com/articles/22453

Webster, Mary E. *The Federalist Papers: In Modern Language Indexed for Today's Political Issues.* Bellevue, WA.: Merril Press, 1999.

White, Morton. *Philosophy, The Federalist, and the Constitution*, New York: 1987.

Zebra Edition. *The Federalist Papers: (Or, How Government is Supposed to Work), Edited for Readability.* Oakesdale, WA: Lucky Zebra Press, 2007.

Pollock, John (1903). *The Popish Plot: a study in the history of the reign of Charles II.* London: Duckworth and Co.

Alan Marshall, 'Oates, Titus (1649–1705)', Oxford Dictionary of National Biography, Oxford University Press, Sept 2004

Oates's Plot". *Catholic Encyclopedia.* New York: Robert Appleton Company. 1913.

Kenyon, J. P. (2000) [1972]. *The Popish Plot.* Reissue of the 1984 Pelican paperback. Phoenix Press.

Alan Marshall, 'Tonge, Israel (1621–1680)', Oxford Dictionary of National Biography, Oxford University Press, Sept 2004

Pincus, Steve (2009). *1688: The First Modern Revolution*. New Haven and London: Yale University Press.; p. 153.

- F. B. Goodrich, *The Court of Napoleon III*. Philadelphia, 1864.
- E. L. Didier, *Life and Letters of Madame Bonaparte*. New York, 1879.
- M. Farquhar, *Foolishly Forgotten Americans*. New York, 2008.
- Charlene M. Boyer Lewis, *Elizabeth Patterson Bonaparte: An American Aristocrat in the Early Republic*. Philadelphia: University of Pennsylvania Press, 2012.
- Berkin, Carol (2014). *Wondrous beauty : the life and adventures of Elizabeth Patterson Bonaparte* (First ed.). New York: Alfred A. Knopf. ISBN 9780307592781. LCCN 2013015270.
- Edward C. Papenfuse, Maryland State Archives. Maryland Tax Exempt Bonds: The Case of Betsy Patterson, 1868-1882. 2007.
- Bacon, Edwin M., ed. (1896). *Supplement to the Acts and Resolves of Massachusetts*. Boston: Geo. Ellis. OCLC 14050329. Retrieved 2009-08-26.
- Feer, Robert (September 1969). "Shays's Rebellion and the Constitution: A Study in Causation". *The New England Quarterly* (Volume 42, No. 3). JSTOR 363616.
- Foner, Eric (2006). *Give Me Liberty! An American History*. New York: W.W Norton. ISBN 978-0-393-92782-5. OCLC 61479662.
- Holland, Josiah Gilbert (1855). *History of Western Massachusetts*. Springfield, MA: S. Bowles. OCLC 505288328.
- Lodge, Henry Cabot (1889). *American Statesmen: George Washington*. Houghton, Mifflin. OCLC 123204544.

- Manuel, Frank Edward; Manuel, Fritzie Prigohzy (2004). *James Bowdoin and the Patriot Philosophers*. Philadelphia: American Philosophical Society. ISBN 978-0-87169-247-4. OCLC 231993575.
- Morse, Anson. *The Federalist Party in Massachusetts to the Year 1800*. Princeton, NJ: Princeton University Press. OCLC 718724.
- North, Gary (Feb 9, 2004). "John Hancock's Big Toe and the Constitution". LewRockwell.com. Retrieved 21 January 2013.
- Richards, Leonard L (2002). *Shays's Rebellion: The American Revolution's Final Battle*. Philadelphia: University of Pennsylvania Press. ISBN 978-0-8122-1870-1. OCLC 56029217.
- Swift, Esther M. (1969). *West Springfield Massachusetts: A Town History*. Springfield, MA: F. A. Bassette Company. OCLC 69843.
- Szatmary, David P. (1980). *Shays's Rebellion: The Making of an Agrarian Insurrection*. University of Massachusetts Press. ISBN 978-0-87023-419-4.
- Zinn, Howard (2005). *A People's History of the United States*. New York: HarperCollins. ISBN 978-0-06-083865-2. OCLC 61265580.
- Beard, Charles (1935). *An Economic Interpretation of the Constitution of the United States*. New York: Macmillan.
- Gross, Robert A. "A Yankee Rebellion? The Regulators, New England, and the New Nation," *New England Quarterly* (2009) 82#1 pp. 112–135 in JSTOR
- Gross, Robert A., ed. (1993). *In Debt to Shays: The Bicentennial of an Agrarian Rebellion*. University Press of Virginia. ISBN 978-0-8139-1354-4.
- Hale, Edward Everett (1891). *The Story of Massachusetts*. Boston: D. Lothrop Company.

- Kaufman, Martin, ed. (1987). *Shays's Rebellion: Selected Essays.* Westfield, MA: Westfield State College. OCLC 15339286.
- McCarthy, Timothy Patrick; McMillan, John, eds. (2011). *The Radical Reader: A Documentary History of the American Radical Tradition.* New York: New Press. ISBN 978-1-59558-742-8. OCLC 741491899. (Reprints a petition to the state legislature.)
- Middleton, Lamar (1968) [1938]. *Revolt, USA.* Freeport, NY: Books for Libraries Press. OCLC 422400.
- Minot, George Richards (1788). *History of the Insurrections in Massachusetts.* Worcester, MA: Isaiah Thomas. OCLC 225355026. (The earliest account of the rebellion. Although this account was deeply unsympathetic to the rural Regulators, it became the basis for most subsequent tellings, including the many mentions of the rebellion in Massachusetts town and state histories.)
- Munroe, James Phinney (1915). *New England Conscience: With Typical Examples.* Boston: R. G. Badger. OCLC 1113783.
- Shattuck, Gary, *Artful and Designing Men: The Trials of Job Shattuck and the Regulation of 1786-1787.* Mustang, OK: Tate Publishing, 2013. ISBN 978-1-62746-575-5
- Starkey, Marion Lena (1955). *A Little Rebellion.* New York: Knopf. OCLC 1513271.
- Wier, Robert (2007). "Shays' Rebellion". In Wier, Robert. *Class in America: Q-Z.* Westport, CT: Greenwood Publishing Group. ISBN 978-0-313-34245-5. OCLC 255745185.
- Bellamy, Edward (1900). *The Duke of Stockbridge: A Romance of Shays' Rebellion.* New York, Boston, and Chicago: Silver, Burdett & Co. OCLC 656929797. (Fictional depiction of the rebellion, as social commentary.)

- Collier, James Lincoln; Collier, Christopher (1978). *The Winter Hero*. Four Winds Press. (The rebellion is the central story of this children's novel.)
- Degenhard, William (1943). *The Regulators*. New York: The Dial Press. OCLC 1663869.
- Martin, William (2007). *The Lost Constitution*. (The rebellion plays a central role in this novel.)

About the Author

None of your fucking business (just kidding). But, still, none of your fucking business.

Dedication

To every citizen of the United States of America and the document that makes this country the greatest social experiment in the history of the world. The United States Constitution.

www.ingramcontent.com/pod-product-compliance
Lightning Source LLC
Chambersburg PA
CBHW060453290526
45791CB00001B/102